CLOUD DEFENSE

ADVANCED ENDPOINT PROTECTION AND SECURE NETWORK STRATEGIES

4 BOOKS IN 1

BOOK 1
FOUNDATIONS OF SECURE NETWORK ARCHITECTURE: DESIGNING RESILIENT NETWORKS FOR THE CLOUD ERA

BOOK 2
MASTERING ENDPOINT PROTECTION: SECURING DEVICES AGAINST MODERN THREATS

BOOK 3
DEFENDING THE CLOUD PERIMETER: BEST PRACTICES FOR CLOUD-BASED NETWORK SECURITY

BOOK 4
THREAT DETECTION AND INCIDENT RESPONSE: PROACTIVE DEFENSE STRATEGIES FOR CYBER THREATS

ROB BOTWRIGHT

Published by Rob Botwright
Library of Congress Cataloging-in-Publication Data
ISBN 978-1-83938-934-4
Cover design by Rizzo

Disclaimer

The contents of this book are based on extensive research and the best available historical sources. However, the author and publisher make no claims, promises, or guarantees about the accuracy, completeness, or adequacy of the information contained herein. The information in this book is provided on an "as is" basis, and the author and publisher disclaim any and all liability for any errors, omissions, or inaccuracies in the information or for any actions taken in reliance on such information. The opinions and views expressed in this book are those of the author and do not necessarily reflect the official policy or position of any organization or individual mentioned in this book. Any reference to specific people, places, or events is intended only to provide historical context and is not intended to defame or malign any group, individual, or entity. The information in this book is intended for educational and entertainment purposes only. It is not intended to be a substitute for professional advice or judgment. Readers are encouraged to conduct their own research and to seek professional advice where appropriate. Every effort has been made to obtain necessary permissions and acknowledgments for all images and other copyrighted material used in this book. Any errors or omissions in this regard are unintentional, and the author and publisher will correct them in future editions.

BOOK 1 - FOUNDATIONS OF SECURE NETWORK ARCHITECTURE: DESIGNING RESILIENT NETWORKS FOR THE CLOUD ERA

BOOK 2 - MASTERING ENDPOINT PROTECTION: SECURING DEVICES AGAINST MODERN THREATS

BOOK 3 - DEFENDING THE CLOUD PERIMETER: BEST PRACTICES FOR CLOUD-BASED NETWORK SECURITY

BOOK 4 - THREAT DETECTION AND INCIDENT RESPONSE: PROACTIVE DEFENSE STRATEGIES FOR CYBER THREATS

Introduction

In the modern era of digital transformation, the way organizations build, manage, and secure their networks has changed dramatically. The shift to cloud-native infrastructure, remote workforces, distributed applications, and hybrid environments has expanded the attack surface and introduced new complexities that traditional security models were never designed to handle. As a result, cybersecurity is no longer a matter of defending static perimeters—it requires dynamic, multi-layered defense strategies that span users, devices, data, and the networks that connect them.

Cloud Defense: Advanced Endpoint Protection and Secure Network Strategies is a comprehensive four-part series designed to equip cybersecurity professionals, architects, and IT leaders with the knowledge and tools required to defend modern digital environments. This collection goes beyond theory and dives deep into the practical aspects of securing the most critical layers of today's infrastructure— from endpoint protection and network design to cloud perimeter defense and threat detection.

Book 1 – Foundations of Secure Network Architecture: Designing Resilient Networks for the Cloud Era lays the strategic groundwork for secure infrastructure. It explores how to architect networks that are both scalable and secure, emphasizing identity-centric design, segmentation, encryption, and cloud-native controls. In a world where infrastructure is elastic and services are distributed, strong architectural principles become the bedrock of cybersecurity.

Book 2 – Mastering Endpoint Protection: Securing Devices Against Modern Threats focuses on the evolving challenges at the edge, where users interact with systems and attackers often gain their first foothold. This book covers endpoint hardening, behavioral defense, EDR technologies, mobile device security, and the policies needed to manage a diverse array of corporate and BYOD endpoints. It presents a layered approach to endpoint security that reflects the sophistication of modern adversaries.

Book 3 – Defending the Cloud Perimeter: Best Practices for Cloud-Based Network Security addresses the complexities of securing cloud environments, where perimeters are fluid and access is identity-driven. It examines the principles of zero trust, secure connectivity, microsegmentation, cloud-native firewalls, and API security. Whether working in a single-cloud, multi-cloud, or hybrid scenario, this book provides the guidance needed to implement effective controls across platforms.

Book 4 – Threat Detection and Incident Response: Proactive Defense Strategies for Cyber Threats brings focus to what happens when prevention isn't enough. No system is invulnerable, and this book emphasizes how to prepare for, detect, and respond to security incidents with speed and precision. Covering everything from SIEM and SOAR integration to threat hunting, containment, and recovery planning, it provides a tactical view of building responsive and resilient security operations.

This series is built for practitioners who understand that cybersecurity is an ongoing effort—not a set-it-and-forget-it exercise. Each book provides practical guidance, real-world examples, and actionable strategies that can be applied across industries and technical landscapes. Whether you're designing a secure network architecture, deploying advanced endpoint controls, managing cloud infrastructure, or leading incident response efforts, *Cloud Defense* is a blueprint for building strong defenses in an era of constant change.

The threats may be sophisticated, but so too can be your defenses. This is your guide to building them.

BOOK 1
FOUNDATIONS OF SECURE NETWORK
ARCHITECTURE DESIGNING RESILIENT NETWORKS
FOR THE CLOUD ERA

ROB BOTWRIGHT

Chapter 1: The New Network Reality

The evolution of modern networks has fundamentally transformed the way organizations approach security. Traditional perimeter-based security models, which once relied on well-defined boundaries and centralized infrastructure, are no longer sufficient in a landscape dominated by remote workforces, cloud computing, mobile endpoints, and increasingly sophisticated cyber threats. The rise of hybrid and multi-cloud environments has dissolved the notion of a single, defensible edge, replacing it with a more complex and fragmented ecosystem where data, users, and resources reside across distributed platforms and locations. This decentralization introduces new risks and requires a rethinking of long-held security assumptions, practices, and architectural frameworks.

In the past, IT environments operated within relatively static parameters. Users logged into machines on-premises, data was stored in centralized data centers, and traffic flowed through controlled network gateways, such as firewalls and proxies. Network segmentation was physical, access control was often coarse-grained, and security monitoring focused primarily on ingress and egress points. However, the increasing demand for flexibility, scalability, and global accessibility has led organizations to embrace cloud services, software-as-a-service (SaaS) platforms, and remote collaboration tools. These technologies, while beneficial for agility and productivity, have simultaneously expanded the attack surface and exposed vulnerabilities in traditional security postures.

One of the most notable shifts in this new reality is the ubiquity of endpoints. Laptops, smartphones, tablets, and IoT devices now function as integral components of enterprise workflows, often operating outside the direct control of central IT teams. These endpoints regularly connect to both corporate and public networks, interact with cloud-based applications, and store sensitive data locally. Every endpoint represents a potential entry point for threat actors, making endpoint protection a critical pillar of modern network defense. Attackers increasingly exploit weak endpoint configurations, outdated software, and social engineering tactics to gain initial access and establish persistent footholds within networks.

Alongside the rise in endpoint diversity, the adoption of cloud infrastructure has introduced a paradigm shift in how organizations store, manage, and secure their digital assets. Cloud providers offer elastic compute, storage, and networking capabilities, enabling businesses to deploy workloads quickly and cost-effectively. Yet, this convenience comes with shared responsibility. While cloud service providers secure the underlying infrastructure, the responsibility for protecting applications, data, access controls, and configurations remains with the customer. Misconfigurations, such as open storage buckets, excessive permissions, or exposed APIs, are among the leading causes of cloud security breaches and underscore the need for diligent governance and visibility.

The dissolution of the traditional perimeter has given rise to the concept of "perimeterless" security, where protection mechanisms must be embedded throughout the network stack. Security must now travel with the data, extend to the user, and remain context-aware at every interaction point. This has led to widespread interest in Zero Trust Architecture (ZTA), a model that operates on the principle of "never trust, always verify." In a Zero Trust environment, access is granted based on strict identity verification, real-time risk assessment, and continuous monitoring of user behavior and device posture. This granular control helps reduce the risk of lateral movement within networks and limits the blast radius of potential breaches. With network traffic patterns becoming more dynamic and less predictable, visibility and monitoring have become central to effective security operations.

Legacy tools designed to inspect traffic at a centralized perimeter struggle to provide meaningful insight into east-west traffic within cloud environments or encrypted communication between microservices. As a result, modern security strategies must incorporate distributed monitoring, behavioral analytics, and machine learning to detect anomalies and respond to incidents in real time. Logging mechanisms must be robust, centrally correlated, and accessible to security teams regardless of whether assets reside on-premises, in the cloud, or across hybrid configurations.

Another critical aspect of the new network reality is the increasing sophistication and automation of cyber threats. Ransomware, supply chain attacks, and advanced persistent threats (APTs) now employ multi-stage tactics and leverage automation to scale their impact. Threat actors are no longer lone individuals but organized groups with significant resources and clear objectives. Their operations may involve reconnaissance, credential harvesting, lateral movement, and data exfiltration, often unfolding over extended periods. To defend against such adversaries, organizations must implement layered security defenses, threat intelligence integration, and rapid incident response capabilities.

Identity has emerged as the new perimeter. With users accessing resources from a variety of devices and locations, strong identity and access management (IAM) has become a linchpin of secure network operations. Multi-factor authentication (MFA), single sign-on (SSO), conditional access policies, and role-based access controls (RBAC) are essential tools in verifying user legitimacy and enforcing the principle of least privilege. However, identity systems themselves have become targets, and attackers frequently attempt to compromise authentication flows or hijack valid sessions to bypass traditional controls.

In parallel, compliance and regulatory pressures continue to evolve. Laws and frameworks such as GDPR, HIPAA, CCPA, and ISO 27001 impose strict requirements on how data is handled, stored, and protected. Organizations must ensure that their network architectures are not only secure but also auditable and compliant with relevant legal standards. This requires documentation, continuous assessment, and alignment with industry best practices. Security is no longer just an IT concern—it is a fundamental aspect of risk management, corporate governance, and customer trust.

Cultural and organizational shifts also play a significant role in adapting to the new network reality. Security cannot be an afterthought or a bottleneck; it must be integrated into the development lifecycle, infrastructure planning, and business strategy. Collaboration between IT, security, development, and compliance teams is essential for creating resilient systems. Security champions, training programs, and clear communication of risk all contribute to a security-first mindset that empowers employees at every level to participate in the organization's defense.

This reimagining of network security challenges professionals to continuously evolve their skillsets, embrace automation, and adopt a proactive stance. The days of static defenses and one-size-fits-all tools are behind us. What lies ahead is a dynamic, constantly shifting battlefield that demands agility, intelligence, and collaboration at every layer of the digital ecosystem.

Chapter 2: Core Principles of Secure Architecture

Security architecture is built on a foundation of core principles that serve as guiding concepts for designing, implementing, and maintaining systems that can withstand modern threats. These principles do not depend on specific technologies or vendors but instead provide a strategic mindset that helps ensure a consistent, risk-aware approach across all layers of infrastructure. Among the most fundamental principles are confidentiality, integrity, and availability—collectively known as the CIA triad. These three pillars form the basis for nearly all security goals and controls. Confidentiality ensures that sensitive information is accessible only to authorized individuals or systems, and is protected from unauthorized disclosure. This principle often relies on strong encryption, access controls, and user authentication. Integrity refers to the accuracy and trustworthiness of data and systems. It ensures that information has not been altered or tampered with, either in transit or at rest, and supports mechanisms such as hashing, digital signatures, and checksums. Availability means that systems and data are accessible to users when needed, which requires redundancy, disaster recovery planning, and protections against denial-of-service attacks.

Beyond the CIA triad, security architecture must also incorporate the principle of least privilege. This concept dictates that users, devices, and applications should be granted the minimum level of access required to perform their tasks—no more and no less. Minimizing privileges reduces the attack surface and limits the potential damage of a compromised account or system. This is especially important in modern networks where users often span different roles, work remotely, and access cloud-based services. Implementing least privilege effectively requires role-based access control (RBAC), fine-grained policies, and continuous monitoring of access patterns to detect anomalies.

Another key principle is defense in depth. This approach recognizes that no single security control is foolproof and that layered defenses are essential to protecting systems against a wide range of threats. By implementing multiple overlapping security controls at different levels—such as network firewalls, endpoint protection, intrusion detection systems, encryption, and user behavior analytics—organizations create redundancies that make it more difficult for attackers to achieve their objectives. Defense in depth also helps absorb failures; if one control fails or is bypassed, others are in place to detect or block the intrusion.

Separation of duties is a critical control for preventing fraud and errors, particularly in environments where administrative access is powerful and sensitive. By ensuring that no single individual has control over all aspects of a critical process—such as approving, executing, and auditing changes—organizations can reduce the risk of insider threats and increase accountability. For example, a system administrator might be able to deploy a server but not configure its security settings without oversight. This principle can be extended through technical means such as role separation, approval workflows, and access audits.

Fail-safe defaults, also known as secure defaults, reflect the idea that systems should be configured to deny access by default unless explicitly allowed. Open configurations, permissive firewalls, or unvalidated inputs often become vulnerabilities because they assume a benign environment. A fail-safe design starts with the assumption that threats are omnipresent and access should be granted only under specific, verified conditions. This principle applies to network ACLs, user permissions, software features, and system APIs. A related concept is minimizing the attack surface, which involves reducing the number of potential entry points by disabling unused services, closing unnecessary ports, and removing unneeded software.

Accountability and traceability are also foundational to secure architecture. Every action within a system should be attributable to an authenticated identity, and there should be a reliable audit trail of activity. Logging and monitoring solutions should capture meaningful events in a tamper-resistant manner, enabling incident detection, forensic investigation, and compliance reporting. Without accountability, malicious actions can go undetected or be misattributed, making response and recovery difficult.

Resilience is another critical consideration. Secure architecture must not only protect against threats but also remain operational and recover gracefully under adverse conditions. This includes hardware failures, software bugs, misconfigurations, and cyberattacks. Building resilience requires redundancy, fault tolerance, regular testing, and automated recovery mechanisms. Backup systems, high-availability clusters, and geographically distributed infrastructure are all methods used to achieve resilience at different scales.

Security must also be embedded into the lifecycle of systems, from initial design to deployment and maintenance. This is known as secure-by-design, a proactive approach that integrates security from the beginning rather than treating it as an afterthought. Secure development practices, code reviews, threat modeling, and automated security testing contribute to early identification of flaws and reduce long-term risks. By addressing vulnerabilities before systems go live, organizations can avoid costly remediations and reputational damage.

Each of these principles supports the creation of a secure architecture that adapts to evolving threats, aligns with business goals, and operates effectively in complex, distributed environments. Applying these principles consistently across networks, endpoints, cloud services, and applications helps establish a security posture that is proactive, resilient, and responsive to change.

Chapter 3: Designing with Zero Trust in Mind

Secure architecture is grounded in a set of foundational principles that guide the design and implementation of systems resilient to compromise, disruption, and unauthorized access. These principles serve as a strategic framework for building defenses that can adapt to a constantly evolving threat landscape. The most widely recognized foundational model is the CIA triad—confidentiality, integrity, and availability. These three components define the essential goals of cybersecurity. Confidentiality refers to protecting sensitive information from being accessed or disclosed to unauthorized parties, typically through encryption, access controls, and strong authentication mechanisms. Integrity ensures that data remains accurate, consistent, and trustworthy over its entire lifecycle, requiring safeguards like hashing, digital signatures, and tamper-evident logs. Availability guarantees that systems, services, and data remain accessible and functional when needed, which is critical for maintaining business continuity and user trust. This involves redundancy, load balancing, and protections against denial-of-service attacks or infrastructure failures.

Another cornerstone of secure architecture is the principle of least privilege, which dictates that users, processes, and systems should be granted only the minimum access rights necessary to perform their required functions. Enforcing this principle significantly reduces the risk of privilege escalation, data leakage, and internal misuse. Implementation often includes role-based access control (RBAC), attribute-based access control (ABAC), and regular audits of access permissions to detect and remove unnecessary or outdated privileges. Least privilege is closely related to the principle of need-to-know, where access to sensitive data is granted only to individuals whose roles specifically require it.

Defense in depth is a layered security approach that assumes any single control could fail and compensates by deploying multiple, overlapping security mechanisms at different layers of the architecture. These layers typically include physical security, network security, application security, endpoint security, and user education. The idea is to delay, detect, and contain attackers at various stages of the attack lifecycle, increasing the likelihood of detection and decreasing the chance of a successful breach. Defense in depth also supports redundancy, allowing certain controls to compensate for failures or blind spots in others. This layered approach is particularly relevant in today's environments, where attackers can move laterally across systems once inside the network perimeter. Fail-safe defaults, or secure-by-default configurations, ensure that systems begin their operation in the most restrictive state possible. Access should be denied unless explicitly granted, services should be disabled unless required, and security features should be enabled by default. This principle counters the common risk posed by insecure default settings, which often go unnoticed in rushed deployments. For example, an exposed API with no authentication, or a storage bucket with public read access, can lead to major data breaches. Designing systems with restrictive defaults encourages thoughtful, deliberate configuration changes and limits exposure out of the box.

The principle of separation of duties helps reduce the likelihood of malicious actions or accidental errors by distributing responsibilities across multiple individuals or systems. No single person should have control over an entire critical process. For instance, one person might develop code, another reviews it, and a third deploys it. This principle introduces accountability and oversight, reducing opportunities for abuse and helping organizations meet compliance standards. In IT environments, separation of duties is implemented through technical role separation, approval workflows, and restricted administrative access.

Chapter 4: Secure Topologies and Network Segmentation

In the context of modern network security, secure topologies and network segmentation are foundational strategies used to limit the spread of threats, control access, and reduce the overall attack surface. A network's topology refers to the arrangement and interconnection of its devices, systems, and communication paths. When designed with security in mind, the topology can act as a structural defense, controlling traffic flow, isolating sensitive resources, and enabling better monitoring. Flat network topologies, where all devices share a common broadcast domain, are simple to deploy but inherently insecure, as they allow lateral movement by attackers once inside the network. In contrast, secure topologies involve segmenting the network into smaller, manageable, and isolated zones, each with defined security controls and limited communication paths.

Network segmentation divides a larger network into subnetworks or zones, each with specific security policies based on function, trust level, or sensitivity. This division can be physical, using separate hardware and cabling, or logical, using virtual LANs

(VLANs), subnets, and access control lists. Logical segmentation is more flexible and cost-effective, especially in environments with complex or dynamic infrastructure. By isolating systems that perform different functions—such as separating user devices from servers, or development environments from production—organizations can better enforce the principle of least privilege and minimize the damage that can be caused by a compromised host. Segmentation also simplifies compliance with regulatory requirements by creating clear boundaries for the storage and processing of sensitive data.

One of the most common implementations of segmentation is the creation of a demilitarized zone (DMZ), which hosts publicly accessible services such as web servers, email gateways, or DNS servers. The DMZ sits between the external internet and the internal network, protected by firewalls that strictly control traffic entering and exiting the zone. This design prevents external attackers from directly accessing the internal network while allowing limited interaction with public-facing services. If a service in the DMZ is compromised, the damage can be contained within that segment without exposing critical internal systems.

Microsegmentation takes this concept further by applying fine-grained controls at the individual workload or application level. Instead of relying solely on perimeter firewalls or VLANs, microsegmentation uses software-defined networking (SDN) or host-based firewalls to enforce policies between workloads, even within the same physical or virtual network. This approach is especially useful in cloud and hybrid environments, where traditional perimeters are blurred and workloads are constantly being spun up, moved, or retired. With microsegmentation, organizations can define communication policies based on identity, tags, or context, ensuring that only authorized and expected interactions occur, regardless of network location.

Network segmentation also enhances visibility and monitoring by concentrating traffic within zones and allowing more targeted inspection. Intrusion detection systems (IDS), data loss prevention (DLP), and other monitoring tools can be strategically placed at the boundaries between segments to watch for suspicious activity or policy violations. In a segmented environment, anomalies such as unauthorized access attempts or data exfiltration can be detected more quickly and with greater precision. The reduced scope of each segment also aids in incident response and containment, as compromised systems can be isolated without affecting the rest of the network.

Implementing secure topologies requires a thorough understanding of the organization's assets, workflows, and communication patterns. Security teams must map out how data flows between systems and identify which assets require protection and which systems must interact. This understanding forms the basis for creating zones with similar security requirements, often referred to as trust zones. For example, a zone containing internal HR systems should not freely communicate with a zone hosting internet-facing applications. Between each zone, enforcement points such as firewalls, routers with ACLs, or next-generation segmentation gateways can apply policies that dictate what kind of traffic is allowed, under what conditions, and by whom.

In addition to static segmentation, dynamic segmentation mechanisms are gaining traction. These use real-time context such as device posture, user identity, or behavioral analysis to adjust network access policies on the fly. For instance, a laptop that connects from an unknown location or fails a security check may be placed in a restricted segment with limited access, while a known, compliant device might be granted broader permissions. Such adaptive models align with Zero Trust principles and enable greater agility in securing modern, distributed environments.

The effectiveness of secure topologies and segmentation depends not only on technical implementation but also on consistent policy management and regular review. As systems are added, removed, or repurposed, segmentation policies must evolve to reflect the current state of the network. Poorly maintained segmentation can lead to over-permissive rules, blind spots, and unmonitored communication paths that attackers can exploit. Therefore, automation and centralized policy orchestration are key to maintaining control, especially in large or dynamic infrastructures. When properly planned and managed, secure network topologies and segmentation offer powerful mechanisms for reducing risk, containing threats, and enabling secure operations in today's complex IT ecosystems.

Chapter 5: Identity-Centric Security Models

Identity-centric security models place identity at the core of network and system access decisions, shifting the focus from traditional perimeter-based defenses to verifying who or what is requesting access, under what circumstances, and with what permissions. As organizations move toward hybrid and cloud environments, where users access resources from various locations and devices, relying solely on network location or IP address as a trust factor has become unreliable. Identity-centric security responds to this reality by treating each access request as potentially untrusted, regardless of where it originates, and by evaluating contextual signals such as user identity, device state, location, and time before granting access. This approach supports a more granular and dynamic security posture, capable of adapting to modern work patterns, decentralized infrastructures, and the growing sophistication of cyber threats.

In an identity-centric model, authentication and authorization processes are foundational. Multi-factor authentication (MFA) is a critical first layer, requiring users to provide more than one form of verification, such as a password and a biometric factor or one-time code. This significantly reduces the effectiveness of stolen credentials, which remain one of the most common methods attackers use to gain unauthorized access. MFA should be enforced not only for external access but also for privileged actions and access to sensitive resources. Single sign-on (SSO) is another component of identity-centric models, allowing users to authenticate once and access multiple systems securely. When integrated with strong authentication protocols and centralized identity management, SSO improves user experience while reducing the number of credentials in circulation.

Identity and Access Management (IAM) systems serve as the backbone of identity-centric security, managing user identities, roles, permissions, and policies across the organization. IAM systems ensure that users are granted the appropriate level of access based on their role, department, or specific business needs, and that this access can be easily adjusted or revoked as circumstances change. Role-based access control (RBAC) and attribute-based access control (ABAC) are key mechanisms in this context. RBAC assigns permissions based on predefined roles, such as "HR Manager" or "Database Administrator," while ABAC evaluates a broader set of attributes—such as user location, time of day, device compliance status, or project assignment—before allowing access. This level of flexibility is essential in dynamic environments where static roles may not sufficiently reflect real-world access needs.

Privileged Access Management (PAM) builds on these concepts by providing additional controls for accounts with elevated permissions, which are high-value targets for attackers. PAM solutions typically include features such as just-in-time access provisioning, session recording, credential vaulting, and automated account rotation. These capabilities reduce the window of opportunity for attackers and limit the potential impact of compromised privileged credentials. In an identity-centric model, privileged access is treated with extreme caution, and every action by a privileged account is logged, monitored, and subject to additional verification.

Federated identity is another key component, especially in environments that span multiple domains, services, or cloud providers. Federation allows organizations to trust and accept identities from external identity providers without requiring local accounts for every user. This enables secure collaboration with partners, contractors, or remote users while maintaining centralized control and auditability. Standards like SAML, OAuth, and

OpenID Connect facilitate secure identity federation and enable seamless integration across platforms.

Context-aware access is increasingly important in identity-centric security, enabling dynamic decisions based on real-time conditions. For instance, access requests from unmanaged or non-compliant devices can be blocked or redirected to remediation portals. Access from unexpected geographic regions or at unusual hours might trigger additional verification or alert the security operations center. These policies can be enforced through Conditional Access, which evaluates the full context of a request—user identity, device health, network location, risk signals—before allowing or denying access. This level of intelligence provides organizations with more control and responsiveness than static access control methods.

Identity-centric models also support Zero Trust principles, which assume that no user or device should be inherently trusted, even if they are inside the network perimeter. Instead, continuous verification is applied, and trust is established per session and per action. This reduces the likelihood of lateral movement within the network if an account or device is compromised. Microsegmentation and identity-aware proxies are used to enforce access at the application level, ensuring that users and devices can only interact with resources they are explicitly authorized to use.

Effective identity management requires ongoing maintenance and visibility. Identity lifecycle management ensures that accounts are created, modified, and deactivated in sync with real-world changes, such as onboarding, role changes, or terminations. Orphaned accounts and excessive permissions must be regularly reviewed and removed to prevent accumulation of risk. Identity governance tools support these processes by automating policy enforcement, conducting periodic access reviews, and generating audit-ready reports. Logging and monitoring of identity-related events are also essential for detecting anomalies and responding to potential breaches. Alerts related to failed logins, account lockouts, or suspicious behavior help identify misuse early and enable prompt action.

Chapter 6: Encryption Everywhere

Encryption everywhere is a guiding principle in modern security architecture that emphasizes the need to protect data at every stage of its lifecycle—at rest, in transit, and in use. In a landscape where sensitive information constantly moves between endpoints, applications, cloud platforms, and storage systems, encryption serves as a critical defense against unauthorized access and data breaches. This approach goes beyond the selective or perimeter-based application of cryptographic controls and assumes that data, regardless of its location or visibility, should be considered a target and protected accordingly. The goal is to render data unintelligible to attackers, even if they manage to intercept it or gain access to storage systems, reducing the potential impact of a compromise.

Data at rest refers to information stored on physical or virtual media, including hard drives, databases, file servers, or cloud storage systems. Encrypting data at rest ensures that even if storage devices are stolen, improperly decommissioned, or accessed by unauthorized individuals, the information remains unreadable without the appropriate decryption keys. Full disk encryption (FDE) and file-level encryption are common methods for securing data at rest. Organizations often use encryption in conjunction with access controls, multi-factor authentication, and key management to create a layered defense. In cloud environments, cloud service providers typically offer encryption for storage services such as block storage, object storage, and database services, with options for either customer-managed or provider-managed keys.

Data in transit refers to information moving across networks, including internal traffic between services, external communications with users, and API requests to cloud platforms. Encrypting data in transit protects it from interception and tampering as it travels over potentially insecure channels such as the internet or public Wi-Fi. Transport Layer Security (TLS) is the standard protocol used to secure data in transit, ensuring that traffic between clients and servers is encrypted and authenticated. Modern best practices enforce HTTPS by default for web services, require TLS for email communication, and secure VPNs or SD-WAN connections for remote access. Internal communications between microservices and distributed components should also be encrypted to prevent exposure in case of lateral movement by an attacker within the network.

Encrypting data in use is a more complex and emerging area of security that focuses on protecting data while it is being processed in memory or actively used by applications. Traditional encryption techniques decrypt data before it can be processed, leaving a window of vulnerability during computation. However, technologies such as homomorphic encryption, secure enclaves, and confidential computing seek to address this challenge by enabling data to remain encrypted even while it is being operated on. While still in early stages for widespread adoption, these techniques are particularly relevant for protecting sensitive workloads in untrusted environments such as public cloud infrastructure or multi-tenant systems.

Key management is an essential component of encryption everywhere, as the security of encrypted data is only as strong as the confidentiality and integrity of the keys used. Proper key management involves generating, storing, rotating, revoking, and auditing cryptographic keys in a secure and compliant manner. Hardware Security Modules (HSMs), Key Management Services (KMS), and integrated solutions offered by cloud providers help organizations manage encryption keys securely and at scale. Best practices include using separate keys for different data types or applications, implementing key usage policies, and logging all key access events for auditing purposes.

Strong encryption relies on well-vetted algorithms and libraries that follow industry standards.

Algorithms such as AES (Advanced Encryption Standard) for symmetric encryption and RSA or ECC (Elliptic Curve Cryptography) for asymmetric encryption are widely accepted due to their proven resistance to attacks. Organizations must avoid using outdated or proprietary algorithms that may contain undiscovered vulnerabilities. Regular cryptographic reviews, updates, and patching of encryption libraries are necessary to stay protected against newly discovered flaws or exploits.

Encryption policies must also be enforced through technical controls and governance frameworks. Data classification plays an important role in determining what data requires encryption, with sensitive or regulated information such as personal data, financial records, and intellectual property receiving the highest levels of protection. Compliance standards like GDPR, HIPAA, PCI DSS, and ISO 27001 often mandate encryption of certain data categories, and failure to comply can result in legal consequences or financial penalties. Encryption everywhere supports regulatory compliance while also strengthening organizational trust and reducing reputational risk.

Chapter 7: Cloud-Native Network Controls

Cloud-native network controls refer to the security mechanisms and configurations designed specifically to protect workloads, applications, and services operating within cloud environments. Unlike traditional on-premises networks, where physical firewalls and static IP ranges dominate, cloud-native networks are highly dynamic, distributed, and abstracted. These environments require a new approach to security—one that is tightly integrated into the cloud provider's architecture, flexible enough to handle constant changes in topology, and capable of enforcing policy at scale. Cloud-native controls leverage software-defined networking (SDN), automation, and identity-aware configurations to provide fine-grained control over traffic flows and access permissions.

At the foundation of cloud-native network security are virtual network components such as Virtual Private Clouds (VPCs), subnets, route tables, and network gateways. These constructs allow organizations to segment cloud resources logically, similar to how VLANs function in traditional networks, but with greater flexibility and automation. Each cloud provider offers its own set of tools and interfaces to manage these components, and secure design requires a deep understanding of how these services interact. Traffic between instances or services is governed not just by IP and port, but also by policies, tags, and identities, which makes it possible to implement microsegmentation and least-privilege access at the network layer.

One of the most critical cloud-native network controls is the use of security groups and network access control lists (NACLs). Security groups act as stateful firewalls attached to compute instances, allowing or denying traffic based on protocol, port, and source or destination. Unlike traditional firewalls, security groups are designed to be highly granular and portable, adapting automatically as instances scale or are replaced. NACLs, on the other hand, operate at the subnet level and are stateless, providing an additional layer of filtering for inbound and outbound traffic. Proper configuration of security groups and NACLs helps enforce strong network boundaries, prevent unintended exposure, and contain lateral movement within cloud environments.

In addition to traffic filtering, cloud-native environments rely heavily on identity-based access controls. Rather than depending solely on IP addresses or device locations, access is often granted based on identity and role. This aligns with the principle of Zero Trust and enables services like AWS IAM roles or Azure Managed Identities to authenticate and authorize communication between services. For example, a serverless function can be configured to access a specific storage bucket only if it presents the correct identity token, removing the need to expose any part of the network publicly. This model significantly reduces the attack surface and mitigates risks associated with hardcoded credentials or overly broad permissions.

Cloud-native controls also extend to perimeter security services such as web application firewalls (WAFs), DDoS protection, and API gateways. These services are designed to protect publicly exposed applications and services from common attack vectors like SQL injection, cross-site scripting, brute-force attacks, and volumetric denial-of-service events. Unlike traditional hardware appliances, cloud-native WAFs are fully managed, scalable, and can be deployed globally within minutes. API gateways provide another crucial layer of control by enforcing authentication, rate limiting, request validation, and routing rules, which is especially important in microservices architectures where APIs are the main interface between components.

Visibility and observability are core components of cloud-native security. Native logging and monitoring tools such as AWS VPC Flow Logs, Azure Network Watcher, and Google Cloud's VPC Service Controls allow security teams to inspect and analyze traffic patterns, detect anomalies, and investigate incidents. These tools generate telemetry data that can be integrated with security information and event management (SIEM) systems or used for automated threat detection. Monitoring traffic flow in cloud environments is essential because it enables organizations to verify that segmentation and access policies are working as intended, and that there is no unauthorized lateral movement or data exfiltration occurring across zones.

Automation and infrastructure as code (IaC) are also fundamental to enforcing cloud-native network controls. With tools like Terraform, CloudFormation, or Bicep, organizations can codify their security policies and deploy consistent, repeatable configurations across multiple environments. This reduces the likelihood of human error and ensures that all resources are provisioned with the correct network controls from the outset. Configuration drift can be monitored and corrected automatically, maintaining a strong security posture even in fast-changing development environments.

Cloud-native controls also incorporate service meshes, which provide a secure way to manage communication between microservices. Service meshes such as Istio or Linkerd abstract network communication and introduce features like mutual TLS, traffic encryption, policy enforcement, and observability at the application level. These capabilities ensure that traffic between internal services is authenticated and encrypted, even when operating within the same network or cluster. This model adds another layer of defense and supports Zero Trust principles by treating every service interaction as potentially untrusted unless verified.

As cloud environments continue to scale and evolve, the role of native controls becomes increasingly vital. Their integration into the fabric of cloud infrastructure enables organizations to implement security that is both adaptive and enforceable, without sacrificing the agility and scalability that make the cloud attractive in the first place.

Chapter 8: Hybrid and Multi-Cloud Security Challenges

Hybrid and multi-cloud environments have become increasingly common as organizations seek flexibility, cost optimization, and vendor diversity in their IT strategies. A hybrid cloud combines on-premises infrastructure with public or private cloud services, while a multi-cloud strategy involves the use of two or more cloud service providers to distribute workloads, data, and services. While these models offer many operational and strategic benefits, they also introduce significant security challenges due to the complexity, variability, and lack of uniform control across environments. One of the primary challenges in hybrid and multi-cloud security is the inconsistency in security policies, tools, and configurations. Each cloud provider has its own terminology, identity management system, logging format, access controls, and encryption standards. Managing security across disparate platforms often requires teams to juggle multiple consoles, APIs, and policy engines, which increases the risk of misconfigurations and policy gaps.

Identity and access management becomes especially complicated in hybrid and multi-cloud settings. Maintaining a consistent identity across cloud and on-prem environments requires integrating directory services, synchronizing user accounts, and enforcing uniform access policies. When multiple identity providers or federation methods are used, it becomes harder to track and enforce least privilege access, monitor user behavior, and detect anomalies. Differences in access control models—such as role-based access control (RBAC) in one environment and attribute-based access control (ABAC) in another—further complicate policy enforcement. Ensuring that identities are properly provisioned, monitored, and deprovisioned across all platforms is essential to reducing the attack surface.

Visibility is another major concern in hybrid and multi-cloud environments. With assets spread across various networks and providers, gaining comprehensive and real-time insight into traffic flows, user activities, and system configurations is a constant challenge. Traditional security tools designed for on-premise environments often lack the integration capabilities needed to pull telemetry data from multiple clouds. As a result, organizations must adopt cloud-native monitoring solutions, logging services, and APIs to gather and correlate security data across platforms. Inadequate visibility can lead to blind spots where attackers can operate undetected, or where policy violations and compliance issues go unnoticed.

Data protection and compliance are also complex in these environments. Sensitive data may be stored in different locations based on workload requirements or data residency laws, making it difficult to apply consistent encryption, backup, and retention policies. Organizations must understand how data is replicated, accessed, and stored across cloud boundaries to avoid unintentional exposure or regulatory noncompliance. Encryption key management becomes more complex when dealing with multiple cloud providers, especially if the organization uses a mix of customer-managed and provider-managed keys. Centralizing key management or using external key management systems may offer more control, but can introduce additional integration challenges.

Another issue in hybrid and multi-cloud environments is the difficulty of maintaining consistent network security controls. Each cloud provider offers its own set of networking tools, such as security groups, firewalls, and routing policies, which may differ significantly in capabilities and configuration. Ensuring uniform segmentation, traffic filtering, and policy enforcement requires abstracting network controls into a unified management layer or deploying third-party security solutions that span multiple platforms. Without standardization, inconsistencies can arise, leading to unintended exposure or poorly isolated resources.

Incident response is further complicated by the need to coordinate across multiple systems and service providers. Detecting, analyzing, and containing a security event in a hybrid or multi-cloud setting requires access to logs, alerts, and system data from all involved platforms. Differences in log formats, alert mechanisms, and time synchronization can hinder investigation and delay remediation. Automation and orchestration tools can help standardize response actions, but they must be carefully designed to function across environments with different APIs and capabilities. Response plans must include cross-cloud playbooks and be regularly tested to ensure they account for the complexities of a distributed infrastructure.

Managing third-party risks also becomes more challenging in a multi-cloud strategy, where each cloud provider may have its own ecosystem of services, tools, and dependencies. The use of cloud-based APIs, SaaS integrations, and platform services increases the organization's exposure to supply chain attacks and vulnerabilities in third-party software. Security assessments, vendor risk management, and continuous monitoring are necessary to evaluate and mitigate these risks, but they require cooperation from multiple providers and transparency into their security practices. Maintaining control while leveraging diverse cloud services demands a balance between decentralization and unified oversight. The lack of shared visibility and standardized security postures often leads to inconsistent enforcement of controls, especially when development teams have autonomy over their own cloud environments or accounts.

Chapter 9: Monitoring, Logging, and Visibility

Monitoring, logging, and visibility are critical components of any modern security architecture, providing the foundation for detecting threats, investigating incidents, and ensuring policy enforcement across networks, systems, and applications. In increasingly complex environments—spanning on-premises infrastructure, cloud platforms, and distributed endpoints—maintaining comprehensive visibility is essential for identifying suspicious activity, understanding system behavior, and validating the effectiveness of security controls. Without proper monitoring and logging, even the most advanced defenses can be rendered ineffective, as threats may go unnoticed or lack the context required for an adequate response. Visibility allows security teams to observe patterns, detect anomalies, and proactively mitigate risks before they escalate into full-blown incidents.

Effective monitoring begins with understanding what needs to be observed. This includes network traffic, system logs, application behavior, user activity, authentication events, and changes to configurations or permissions. Network-level monitoring provides insight into communication between devices, helping identify unauthorized access attempts, data exfiltration, or lateral movement within the environment. Tools such as intrusion detection systems (IDS), network traffic analysis (NTA) platforms, and flow logging services are used to capture and evaluate this data in real time. Monitoring at the system and application level offers additional layers of detail, revealing events such as failed logins, suspicious file access, privilege escalation, and unexpected process execution. These signals can indicate compromise or misuse, and they must be collected consistently across diverse environments.

Logging is the process of recording events and actions that occur within systems and applications. Proper logging enables organizations to maintain an auditable trail of activity, essential for forensic analysis, compliance reporting, and performance troubleshooting. Logs must be generated in a structured format, time-stamped, and stored in a secure and tamper-evident manner to preserve integrity and utility. Logs should capture both successful and failed actions to provide a complete picture of system behavior. This includes authentication logs, access logs, audit trails, system events, error messages, and administrative actions. A common challenge in logging is the overwhelming volume of data generated, especially in large-scale or cloud-native environments. To address this, organizations must implement logging policies that define what should be logged, at what granularity, and for how long logs should be retained.

Centralized log management is critical to achieving meaningful visibility and effective incident response. Without centralization, logs remain fragmented across devices, applications, and services, making correlation and analysis difficult. Security Information and Event Management (SIEM) systems play a key role in aggregating log data, parsing it into a consistent format, and enabling rule-based detection, alerting, and reporting. SIEM solutions integrate with a wide variety of data sources, providing a unified view of security-relevant activity across the organization. They support real-time correlation of events, threat intelligence integration, and custom detection logic tailored to the organization's risk profile. For cloud environments, native services such as AWS CloudTrail, Azure Monitor, and Google Cloud Audit Logs offer telemetry specific to each platform, and must be integrated with centralized monitoring infrastructure to avoid visibility gaps.

Visibility also extends to user activity and endpoint behavior. Endpoint Detection and Response (EDR) platforms provide telemetry from endpoints, capturing detailed data on process execution, file changes, registry modifications, and network connections. This information is crucial for detecting malware, identifying compromised devices, and performing root cause analysis during investigations. User behavior analytics (UBA) adds another layer, using machine learning to baseline normal activity and detect deviations that may indicate insider threats, account takeover, or credential abuse. These behavioral indicators are especially valuable in identifying sophisticated attacks that bypass traditional signature-based defenses.

Cloud-native environments introduce additional visibility challenges, as services are ephemeral, infrastructure is dynamic, and control planes are abstracted from the user. Monitoring must therefore include orchestration layers such as Kubernetes, serverless functions, and containerized workloads. Observability tools designed for these environments collect metrics, traces, and logs to provide real-time insights into performance and security. Tools such as Prometheus, Grafana, Fluentd, and OpenTelemetry help developers and security teams understand how applications behave under different conditions, enabling early detection of issues and efficient debugging.

Monitoring and visibility are only effective if they drive action. Alert fatigue, misconfigured thresholds, and irrelevant logs can lead to missed signals and delayed response. To address this, security teams must tune alerting rules, prioritize actionable events, and incorporate context such as asset value, threat intelligence, and user risk scores. Automation through Security Orchestration, Automation, and Response (SOAR) platforms helps reduce manual effort, improve response times, and enforce consistency in handling incidents. Continuous refinement of monitoring configurations, periodic audits of logging coverage, and regular validation of visibility tools are necessary to ensure alignment with evolving threats and organizational needs.

Chapter 10: Future-Proofing Your Network

Future-proofing your network involves designing, implementing, and maintaining infrastructure that can adapt to evolving business needs, emerging technologies, and the ever-changing threat landscape. This approach requires strategic planning and technical foresight to ensure that the network remains resilient, scalable, secure, and capable of integrating new capabilities as they arise. As organizations continue to adopt hybrid work models, expand into multi-cloud environments, and rely heavily on digital services, network infrastructure must be built with the flexibility to support rapid growth, unexpected shifts in usage patterns, and unforeseen security challenges. A future-proof network must be able to scale both horizontally and vertically, allowing for increased bandwidth demands, device proliferation, and the integration of new services without requiring a complete architectural overhaul.

Scalability begins with modular network design. Using a modular approach enables organizations to add or upgrade components without disrupting core services. This includes scalable routing and switching architectures, virtualized network functions, and cloud-native connectivity models that allow seamless expansion across data centers and cloud regions. Virtualization technologies such as network function virtualization (NFV) and software-defined networking (SDN) provide the abstraction necessary to decouple hardware from services, offering the agility to reconfigure, optimize, and automate networks through software without relying on costly physical deployments. This software-driven model is essential for supporting digital transformation initiatives and rapidly changing business requirements.

Automation is another core element of a future-proof network. Manual configuration and maintenance are not sustainable in environments where services are continuously deployed and updated. Infrastructure as Code (IaC) tools such as Terraform and Ansible allow for the automated deployment and configuration of network resources, ensuring consistency, repeatability, and speed. Automation reduces human error, accelerates change management, and allows security policies and network configurations to be version-controlled, tested, and rolled back if necessary. Event-driven automation enables real-time response to network conditions or threats, adjusting configurations dynamically to maintain performance and security.

Security must be embedded into the network at every level to ensure that it can defend against both current and future threats. This includes the integration of Zero Trust principles, which assume that no device, user, or workload is inherently trusted and that access must be continuously verified. Zero Trust network architectures enforce strict access controls, microsegmentation, and real-time policy evaluation based on user identity, device posture, and contextual risk. Encrypted traffic inspection, behavioral analytics, and identity-aware firewalls contribute to a proactive security model that evolves with the threat landscape. Future-proof security also depends on central visibility, advanced telemetry, and AI-powered threat detection, all of which are necessary for defending against sophisticated and persistent adversaries.

Resilience is another essential attribute of a future-ready network. Network designs must include redundancy at critical points, diverse failover paths, and automatic recovery mechanisms to minimize downtime and ensure business continuity. Load balancing, high availability configurations, and distributed architectures help ensure that traffic can be rerouted or scaled across multiple locations during peak demand or failure scenarios. Regular stress testing, disaster recovery drills, and chaos engineering practices can validate the robustness of the network and highlight potential points of failure before they are exploited or cause business disruption.

Cloud-native connectivity plays an increasingly important role in future-proofing networks, particularly as organizations adopt hybrid and multi-cloud models. Integrating cloud provider-specific networking capabilities—such as AWS Transit Gateway, Azure Virtual WAN, or Google Cloud VPC—into core network strategies allows for secure, optimized, and globally distributed access to cloud resources. Interconnects, direct peering, and edge networking solutions enable low-latency, high-throughput communication between environments and users, whether they are in corporate offices, data centers, or working remotely. Cloud-native security and monitoring tools provide the necessary insight and control to maintain visibility and enforce consistent policies across platforms.

Adaptability is also key, and networks must be designed with change in mind. Supporting emerging technologies such as 5G, edge computing, IoT, and AI-driven analytics requires flexible architectures that can integrate with new protocols, hardware, and data processing models. This includes support for IPv6, container-based networking, programmable interfaces, and network slicing, all of which are critical for future scalability and interoperability. Policies and governance structures must be in place to manage these integrations while maintaining compliance and security. As organizations grow and evolve, a future-proof network becomes not only a technical necessity but a strategic enabler of innovation, agility, and resilience in an increasingly digital world.

BOOK 2
MASTERING ENDPOINT PROTECTION
SECURING DEVICES AGAINST MODERN THREATS

ROB BOTWRIGHT

Chapter 1: The Expanding Attack Surface

The expanding attack surface represents one of the most pressing challenges in cybersecurity today, driven by the rapid adoption of cloud computing, mobile devices, remote work, Internet of Things (IoT), and a growing reliance on digital services. As organizations embrace digital transformation and decentralize their infrastructure, the number of potential entry points for attackers increases exponentially. Every connected endpoint, every application interface, and every user credential represents a possible vulnerability, making it harder for security teams to maintain full visibility and control. Traditional perimeter-based security models are no longer sufficient, as users and data now operate far beyond the boundaries of centralized networks, interacting across a constantly shifting digital ecosystem.

Endpoints have become one of the most targeted areas within this expanding attack surface. With employees using laptops, smartphones, tablets, and even personal devices to access corporate resources, the security perimeter has moved to the individual user. These endpoints often connect from untrusted networks, lack consistent patching, and may run outdated software, making them attractive targets for attackers seeking to establish a foothold. Malware, phishing, and ransomware campaigns frequently exploit endpoint vulnerabilities, often bypassing traditional defenses through social engineering or legitimate-looking attack vectors. Endpoint protection platforms and mobile device management systems help reduce risk, but ensuring consistent configuration and policy enforcement across thousands of distributed devices remains a persistent challenge.

Cloud adoption adds another layer of complexity to the attack surface. As organizations migrate workloads to public and private cloud platforms, security teams must contend with new technologies, shared responsibility models, and dynamic infrastructure. Misconfigured storage buckets, overly permissive IAM roles, exposed APIs, and unsecured cloud services are common vulnerabilities that attackers actively seek out. Unlike traditional environments, where assets and their relationships are relatively static, cloud environments are highly dynamic, with services being created, modified, and decommissioned constantly. This dynamism makes it difficult to maintain up-to-date inventories and enforce consistent security policies, especially when multiple teams have access to create and deploy cloud resources without centralized oversight.

The proliferation of web applications and APIs significantly contributes to the expanding attack surface. Organizations increasingly rely on customer-facing portals, third-party integrations, and microservices architectures to deliver functionality and improve user experience. These interfaces often expose business logic, authentication mechanisms, and backend services to the public internet, increasing the risk of exploitation. Common vulnerabilities such as SQL injection, cross-site scripting (XSS), broken access controls, and insecure API endpoints remain frequent attack vectors. The rapid development cycles of DevOps and agile teams can lead to security being overlooked in the rush to release features, allowing critical flaws to slip into production unnoticed.

The Internet of Things also represents a rapidly growing segment of the attack surface, particularly in sectors like healthcare, manufacturing, and critical infrastructure. IoT devices often operate with limited computing resources, minimal built-in security, and poor patching mechanisms. Many devices are deployed with default credentials, lack encryption, or use outdated protocols, creating easy targets for attackers to exploit. Once compromised, these devices can be used for surveillance, data theft, or as part of a botnet for large-scale attacks such as distributed denial of service (DDoS). The diversity of IoT manufacturers and lack of unified security standards further complicate efforts to secure these environments.

Identity and access management also plays a central role in the expanding attack surface. As more services and users require authentication, the number of credentials in use grows significantly. Weak passwords, reused credentials, and phishing attacks contribute to the increasing prevalence of account takeovers. Threat actors frequently target identity infrastructure such as Active Directory, federation services, and cloud IAM systems to escalate privileges and move laterally within networks. The use of multi-factor authentication, conditional access policies, and identity monitoring helps mitigate risk, but organizations must also focus on securing service accounts, API tokens, and machine identities, which often go unmonitored and unmanaged.

Supply chain vulnerabilities present yet another layer to the attack surface, where organizations may be compromised through their vendors, partners, or third-party software dependencies.

Attacks like SolarWinds demonstrated how attackers can infiltrate trusted software updates and spread malware to thousands of downstream systems. Managing third-party risk requires thorough vetting, continuous monitoring, and contractual obligations for secure development practices, but visibility into these dependencies is often limited. Software components from open-source projects or external libraries can introduce vulnerabilities if not properly reviewed or maintained, adding to the risk.

The shift to remote work has further accelerated the expansion of the attack surface by decentralizing access to critical systems and data. Employees now operate from home networks that are often poorly secured, and personal devices are used in both personal and professional contexts. The increased use of collaboration tools, video conferencing platforms, and remote desktop protocols has opened new vectors for exploitation, often by exploiting unpatched software, misconfigurations, or weak authentication. Without a centralized infrastructure, enforcing consistent security hygiene becomes more difficult, requiring new tools and strategies to monitor, control, and protect remote endpoints and connections.

Chapter 2: Anatomy of an Endpoint Threat

An endpoint threat refers to any attack vector that targets devices such as desktops, laptops, smartphones, tablets, or servers which connect to a network and interact with organizational resources. These endpoints serve as the most direct interface between users and the digital infrastructure of an enterprise, making them prime targets for cyber attackers. Understanding the anatomy of an endpoint threat involves examining the various stages of the attack lifecycle, the techniques employed by threat actors, and the weaknesses they exploit to achieve persistence, data theft, or disruption. Most endpoint threats begin with some form of initial compromise, often through phishing emails, malicious attachments, drive-by downloads, or infected removable media. Social engineering plays a major role in this stage, as attackers aim to trick users into clicking on links, executing malicious code, or entering credentials on fake login pages.

Once the initial compromise is achieved, the attacker's payload is typically delivered and executed. This could be in the form of a trojan, ransomware, keylogger, or remote access trojan (RAT), all of which are designed to establish a foothold on the target device. Attackers often use obfuscation and polymorphism to evade detection by traditional antivirus solutions. The malicious code may also disable or bypass endpoint protection software, modify registry keys, create hidden scheduled tasks, or exploit legitimate administrative tools to mask its presence and activities. Fileless malware is particularly dangerous in this context, as it resides in memory and uses native tools like PowerShell or Windows Management Instrumentation (WMI) to operate, leaving minimal traces on disk and making forensic analysis more difficult.

After establishing a foothold, the threat actor will attempt to escalate privileges. Privilege escalation is critical for gaining broader access to the system and performing actions such as installing kernel-level drivers, accessing protected system files, or pivoting to other systems. Attackers may exploit unpatched vulnerabilities, misconfigured permissions, or use credential harvesting techniques like token impersonation, Mimikatz, or LSASS memory scraping to obtain administrative credentials. With elevated privileges, attackers can disable security controls, exfiltrate data, or move laterally across the network.

Lateral movement is the process by which attackers extend their control from the initially compromised endpoint to other devices or systems within the network. Techniques such as pass-the-hash, remote desktop protocol (RDP) exploitation, and exploitation of trust relationships are commonly used to spread an attack from one endpoint to another. Each new compromised endpoint becomes a launch point for additional attacks, allowing the threat actor to explore the network, identify high-value assets, and maintain persistence. During this phase, attackers may also establish command and control (C2) channels, often encrypted or disguised as legitimate traffic, to maintain communication with compromised endpoints, issue commands, and extract data.

Persistence mechanisms are employed to ensure the attacker can regain access to the system even after reboots or initial detection. Common persistence techniques include modifying system startup processes, installing rootkits, or leveraging legitimate scheduled tasks and services. Some threats install backdoors or secondary payloads, allowing reentry even after primary malware is removed. Advanced threats may also deploy time-triggered payloads or update their code remotely to adapt to security measures.

The final stage of an endpoint threat often involves the execution of the attacker's end goal. This could be data theft, where sensitive files, credentials, or intellectual property are exfiltrated; data encryption and extortion, as seen in ransomware attacks; or even sabotage, where data is corrupted or systems are rendered inoperable. Data exfiltration may occur over encrypted channels, hidden within legitimate traffic, or through cloud-based file transfer tools to evade detection. In some cases, the threat actor may leave behind wipers or destructive payloads designed to erase traces of the attack or inflict maximum damage.

Throughout the entire process, stealth and evasion are key priorities for the attacker. Endpoint threats often involve disabling logging mechanisms, tampering with antivirus or endpoint detection and response (EDR) agents, and clearing event logs. Advanced threats use living-off-the-land techniques, relying on legitimate administrative tools and system processes to blend in with normal activity and avoid raising suspicion. Attackers often test their methods against commonly used endpoint security tools to ensure their payloads will go undetected. The anatomy of an endpoint threat is characterized by a sequence of well-planned actions that exploit human error, software vulnerabilities, and misconfigurations, requiring layered defenses, real-time monitoring, and behavior-based detection to identify and mitigate the threat before it causes significant harm.

Chapter 3: Endpoint Security Fundamentals

Endpoint security fundamentals form the backbone of a strong cybersecurity posture in any organization, as endpoints represent the most commonly targeted entry points for attackers. With the increasing mobility of the workforce, the proliferation of bring-your-own-device (BYOD) policies, and the widespread adoption of cloud services, endpoints have become more exposed than ever before. These devices—ranging from desktops and laptops to smartphones, tablets, and even IoT equipment—serve as critical access points to corporate data and systems, making them attractive targets for malware, phishing, ransomware, and other forms of cyber intrusion. To address this, endpoint security must be approached with a combination of policies, technologies, and controls that aim to prevent, detect, and respond to threats at the device level.

The foundation of endpoint security begins with ensuring that each device is properly configured and hardened before being deployed into a production environment. This involves disabling unnecessary services, closing unused ports, applying security baselines, and enforcing the principle of least privilege. A hardened endpoint is less susceptible to attack because it minimizes the available vectors through which an attacker might gain access. Operating system settings, firmware updates, and BIOS configurations should also be secured to prevent low-level manipulation of the device.

Patch management is another essential component of endpoint security. Vulnerabilities in operating systems and software are frequently discovered and publicly disclosed, often accompanied by proof-of-concept exploits that cybercriminals can weaponize. Regularly applying patches and software updates closes these security gaps and reduces the attack surface. Automated patch management tools can streamline the process and ensure that endpoints are kept up to date without relying on manual intervention, which is particularly important in environments with a high number of remote or geographically distributed devices.

Antivirus and antimalware software have long been the traditional front line of endpoint defense. While signature-based detection remains relevant, modern endpoint protection platforms (EPP) incorporate behavioral analysis, heuristic techniques, and machine learning to identify previously unknown threats. These systems monitor running processes, system calls, and user behavior to detect anomalies that may indicate malicious activity. In many cases, endpoint detection and response (EDR) tools are layered on top of EPP solutions to provide deeper visibility and investigative capabilities. EDR tools can capture detailed telemetry from endpoints, enabling security teams to trace the origins of an attack, analyze its impact, and take appropriate containment actions.

Data protection also plays a vital role in endpoint security fundamentals. Devices often contain sensitive or proprietary information that, if stolen or leaked, can lead to significant financial and reputational damage. Encrypting data at rest on endpoint devices ensures that, even if a device is lost or stolen, its contents remain inaccessible to unauthorized individuals. Full disk encryption, file-level encryption, and the use of hardware-backed security modules such as Trusted Platform Modules (TPMs) help secure local data. Additionally, secure remote wipe capabilities should be in place to enable administrators to erase data from lost or compromised devices.

Access control is another pillar of endpoint security, where the goal is to ensure that only authorized users and systems can access resources. Strong authentication mechanisms, including multi-factor authentication (MFA), help verify user identities and prevent unauthorized access. MFA combines something the user knows (such as a password) with something the user has (like a hardware token or smartphone) or something the user is (such as a fingerprint or facial recognition). Combined with centralized identity and access management (IAM) systems, this approach ensures consistent and enforceable access policies across all endpoints.

Monitoring and logging are necessary for detecting and responding to endpoint threats in real time. Events such as login attempts, software installations, configuration changes, and file access should be logged and analyzed to identify potential indicators of compromise. Security information and event management (SIEM) systems can collect and correlate these logs, alerting security teams to suspicious activity. Additionally, endpoint agents should be capable of initiating automated responses, such as isolating the device from the network, terminating malicious processes, or rolling back changes made by ransomware.

User awareness and training complete the picture by addressing the human element of endpoint security. Even the most sophisticated technical controls can be undermined by a user clicking on a phishing link or downloading a malicious attachment. Regular training on safe computing practices, social engineering tactics, and incident reporting protocols helps empower users to act as the first line of defense. Endpoint security is not just about the technology deployed but also about creating a culture of security across the organization, where both systems and people work together to prevent compromise.

Chapter 4: Antivirus vs. Next-Gen EDR

The evolution of endpoint threats has driven a corresponding evolution in security technologies, leading to a shift from traditional antivirus solutions to more advanced next-generation endpoint detection and response (EDR) platforms. Understanding the difference between antivirus and next-gen EDR is essential for organizations seeking to protect their endpoints in a threat landscape that is increasingly dynamic, stealthy, and sophisticated. Traditional antivirus software was designed to detect and block known malware by using signature-based detection. These signatures are essentially digital fingerprints of malicious files that allow the antivirus engine to identify and neutralize threats it has seen before. While effective against previously encountered malware, this approach is limited in its ability to detect zero-day threats, fileless malware, polymorphic attacks, and other advanced techniques that constantly change their appearance to evade detection.

Antivirus solutions typically run as background services on endpoints, scanning files, emails, and processes for known malicious patterns. They rely heavily on periodic updates from a central signature database to stay current with emerging threats. However, attackers have become adept at modifying code just enough to bypass these static detection mechanisms. Fileless malware, for example, lives in memory and executes using legitimate system tools such as PowerShell or WMI, making it invisible to traditional antivirus programs that scan files on disk. In such scenarios, antivirus software may be blind to the attack entirely, allowing threat actors to compromise systems and exfiltrate data undetected.

Next-generation EDR platforms address these limitations by focusing on behavior-based detection, continuous monitoring, and in-depth visibility into endpoint activity. Rather than looking only for known malware signatures, EDR solutions analyze patterns of behavior that may indicate malicious activity. This includes unusual process execution, privilege escalation, suspicious registry modifications, and lateral movement across the network. By continuously monitoring endpoints for these behavioral indicators, EDR platforms can detect threats that have never been seen before and respond in real time. This proactive approach enables security teams to stop attacks early in their lifecycle, before significant damage is done.

EDR tools also collect and store detailed telemetry from endpoints, such as file access history, process trees, network connections, and user actions. This data is critical for incident investigation and threat hunting, allowing analysts to reconstruct attack timelines, determine root cause, and identify affected systems. Unlike antivirus solutions, which primarily offer automated protection, EDR platforms are designed for use by skilled security professionals who can interpret the collected data and initiate appropriate responses. Many EDR tools include response capabilities such as isolating infected endpoints, terminating malicious processes, or rolling back system changes to pre-infection states.

Another key difference lies in the level of integration and automation offered by EDR platforms. Modern EDR solutions are often part of a broader security ecosystem, integrating with security information and event management (SIEM) systems, threat intelligence feeds, and security orchestration and automation (SOAR) platforms. This integration enables faster detection and response across the organization and supports coordinated action across multiple security layers. For example, a threat detected by the EDR agent on one endpoint can trigger automated containment across all affected devices, alert the SOC team, and initiate an investigation workflow.

While antivirus is generally seen as a basic, standalone protection tool suitable for consumer use or low-risk environments, EDR is better suited for enterprises that require comprehensive endpoint visibility and advanced threat detection capabilities. EDR does not necessarily replace antivirus but rather extends and enhances endpoint protection. In fact, many modern EDR platforms include built-in antivirus functionality, offering signature-based detection alongside behavioral analytics, machine learning, and cloud-based analysis. This layered defense model ensures coverage against both known and unknown threats and provides the agility needed to respond to today's fast-evolving attack methods.

Cost and complexity also differentiate antivirus and EDR. Antivirus is typically easy to deploy and manage with minimal user interaction, while EDR platforms require more technical expertise to configure, tune, and interpret. However, the increased visibility and control provided by EDR can dramatically improve an organization's ability to defend against advanced persistent threats, ransomware, and insider attacks. As threat actors continue to innovate, relying solely on legacy antivirus software leaves critical gaps in protection, making the adoption of next-gen EDR an essential step toward a modern and resilient endpoint security strategy.

Chapter 5: Device Hardening Techniques

Device hardening techniques are a set of proactive measures used to reduce the attack surface of computing devices by eliminating unnecessary functions, securing configurations, and enforcing strict access controls. Hardening is essential because default installations of operating systems and applications often include features and services that are not required in a specific environment, yet can be exploited by attackers if left enabled. The process begins with identifying the device's intended function and determining the minimum software, services, and privileges needed to perform that role. From there, all non-essential components should be disabled or removed to reduce potential points of compromise.

One of the most fundamental device hardening practices is operating system hardening. This includes disabling unused services and protocols such as Telnet, SMBv1, or RDP when they are not required. These legacy protocols often have known vulnerabilities or lack modern security features, making them high-risk if left exposed. In addition, unnecessary user accounts and groups should be removed or disabled, and all default credentials should be changed or eliminated. Secure baseline configurations, often defined by frameworks like CIS Benchmarks or DISA STIGs, provide detailed guidance on how to lock down operating systems according to best practices. These baselines should be applied consistently across all devices, with deviation monitored and corrected.

Patch management is another critical hardening measure. Devices must be kept up to date with security patches for the operating system, firmware, and installed applications. Vulnerabilities in software are frequently discovered and exploited by attackers, often within days of being disclosed. To minimize exposure, patching processes should be automated where possible, prioritized based on severity, and regularly audited to ensure compliance. In cases where immediate patching is not possible due to compatibility or operational constraints, compensating controls such as firewall rules or application whitelisting should be implemented to reduce risk until the patch can be applied.

Access control is a core principle of device hardening. The principle of least privilege dictates that users and processes should only have the minimum permissions necessary to perform their tasks. Local administrative privileges should be removed from standard user accounts, and elevated access should be granted only through controlled methods such as just-in-time access or temporary privilege escalation. Devices should also enforce strong authentication methods, including complex passwords, account lockout policies, and multi-factor authentication (MFA). Secure shell (SSH) access should be protected by public key authentication instead of passwords, and remote access should be restricted to authorized IP addresses or VPN users only.

Application control is another effective device hardening strategy. This involves using whitelisting technologies to allow only approved software to run on a device, thereby preventing unknown or malicious executables from being executed. Application control solutions can be implemented using built-in tools like Microsoft AppLocker or third-party platforms that provide centralized management. Devices should also be monitored for unauthorized software installations or changes in system behavior, as these could indicate a breach or policy violation.

Logging and auditing are essential components of a hardened device. Security-related events such as login attempts, privilege changes, and file access should be logged and regularly reviewed. Logs must be protected from tampering and stored in a central location for analysis and long-term retention. Devices should be configured to send logs to a SIEM platform, where they can be correlated with events from other systems to detect suspicious patterns. In addition, host-based intrusion detection systems (HIDS) and file integrity monitoring tools can alert administrators to unauthorized changes to critical system files or configurations.

Network hardening of endpoints is also vital. Devices should be placed behind firewalls and configured to allow only necessary inbound and outbound communications. Host-based firewalls should be enabled and configured to block unsolicited connections. Secure network protocols such as HTTPS, SSH, and SFTP should replace their insecure counterparts, and unnecessary network shares or discovery protocols should be disabled. DNS settings should point to trusted servers, and DNS over HTTPS (DoH) can be used to encrypt DNS queries.

Physical security cannot be ignored in device hardening, especially for laptops, servers, or devices in publicly accessible locations. Devices should be locked or housed in secure cabinets, BIOS or UEFI settings should be password-protected, and boot order settings should be restricted to prevent unauthorized use of external media. Combined with encryption for data at rest and remote wipe capabilities, physical hardening ensures that stolen or lost devices do not become a data breach risk. Each of these hardening measures, when implemented collectively, builds a layered defense that significantly enhances the security posture of any endpoint or system within the network.

Chapter 6: Policy-Driven Endpoint Control

Policy-driven endpoint control is a strategic approach to securing devices by enforcing predefined rules and configurations that govern how endpoints behave, what they can access, and how they interact with networks and applications. Instead of relying on ad-hoc or manual configurations, organizations implement centralized policies that standardize security controls across all devices, ensuring consistency, compliance, and reduced administrative overhead. This method supports scalability, particularly in environments with large numbers of endpoints spread across multiple locations, where manual oversight would be impractical and prone to error. By leveraging policy-driven control, organizations can automate the enforcement of security best practices and quickly adapt to emerging threats without direct intervention on each device.

One of the core components of policy-driven endpoint control is the use of group policies or mobile device management (MDM) systems to define and distribute settings to endpoints. Group Policy Objects (GPOs) in Windows environments allow administrators to control a wide range of configurations such as password policies, lock screen behavior, removable media usage, and user permissions. For mobile and cross-platform environments, MDM solutions like Microsoft Intune, VMware Workspace ONE, or Jamf allow centralized control over iOS, Android, macOS, and Windows devices. These tools enable enforcement of security baselines, encryption settings, application restrictions, and compliance rules, ensuring that all devices adhere to organizational policies regardless of their location or ownership model.

Access control policies form a critical part of endpoint control, particularly in enforcing the principle of least privilege. Policies define who can log into a device, what privileges they have, and what actions they are allowed to perform. Role-based access control (RBAC) and attribute-based access control (ABAC) can be enforced at the endpoint level to ensure users are only granted access to the data and functions necessary for their roles. This reduces the risk of accidental or malicious misuse of privileges. Policies may also include just-in-time access, where elevated permissions are granted temporarily based on approval workflows and automatically revoked after use, reducing the window of exposure for privileged accounts.

Application control policies are another key aspect, allowing organizations to specify which applications can or cannot run on endpoints. This can be implemented through allowlists and blocklists, where only authorized software is permitted to execute. Tools like Microsoft Defender Application Control (WDAC) or AppLocker enforce these policies, preventing users from installing or running unauthorized applications, including potentially unwanted programs (PUPs) or malware. In environments where users require flexibility, application control policies can be configured to allow trusted vendors or digitally signed applications while still blocking unknown or untrusted executables.

Device control policies focus on managing peripheral access, including USB ports, Bluetooth, CD/DVD drives, and other input/output devices. These controls are essential for preventing data leakage, unauthorized data transfers, or the introduction of malware via removable media. Policies can be configured to block all external storage by default, allow read-only access, or permit access only to encrypted or organization-issued devices. In addition, endpoint security platforms often include features to monitor or alert on the insertion of removable media, providing greater visibility into device usage patterns.

Network access policies further enhance endpoint control by dictating how and when a device can connect to corporate networks or resources. Conditional access policies, often integrated with identity providers and MDM platforms, assess the security posture of a device before granting access to sensitive systems. For example, access may be denied if the device is not encrypted, lacks a recent security update, or fails an antivirus check. Network access control (NAC) solutions extend these policies to physical and wireless networks by validating device compliance before allowing connection, thereby preventing non-compliant or rogue devices from introducing risk.

Compliance policies ensure that endpoints maintain an acceptable level of security at all times. These policies continuously evaluate device health and configuration status, triggering remediation actions or access restrictions if a device falls out of compliance. For example, if an endpoint fails to report its antivirus status or has a disabled firewall, it can be automatically quarantined or redirected to a remediation network. Real-time compliance reporting provides administrators with a clear view of the organization's security posture and supports audits and regulatory requirements.

Policy-driven endpoint control supports automation and orchestration by integrating with broader security ecosystems. Events triggered by policy violations can be forwarded to security information and event management (SIEM) systems or trigger workflows in security orchestration, automation, and response (SOAR) platforms. This enables faster detection, triage, and response to endpoint incidents. With the right policies in place, organizations can ensure that endpoints are not only protected but also continuously aligned with evolving business needs and threat landscapes.

Chapter 7: Endpoint Detection and Response (EDR)

Endpoint Detection and Response (EDR) is a modern cybersecurity technology designed to provide continuous monitoring, detection, and response capabilities on endpoint devices such as desktops, laptops, servers, and mobile devices. Unlike traditional antivirus software that focuses primarily on preventing known threats using signature-based detection, EDR systems are built to identify suspicious behavior, investigate security incidents, and respond to advanced threats that may have bypassed preventative defenses. EDR platforms collect and store vast amounts of endpoint telemetry, including information about processes, file activity, registry changes, network connections, user behavior, and system events. This data is analyzed in real time and retrospectively to detect indicators of compromise (IOCs) and indicators of attack (IOAs), allowing security teams to respond swiftly and with precision.

At the core of any EDR solution is the capability to detect malicious or anomalous activity through behavior-based analysis. By establishing baselines of normal activity, the system can flag deviations that may indicate an attack in progress. For instance, if a legitimate process suddenly attempts to connect to an unusual external domain, access sensitive files, or spawn child processes in an uncommon sequence, the EDR tool can generate an alert. These alerts are often prioritized by severity and include contextual details that help analysts understand what happened, when, and how it fits into the broader attack chain. EDR tools typically include visual attack timelines, process trees, and correlation engines that simplify root cause analysis and reduce time to resolution.

One of the most valuable capabilities of EDR platforms is their response functionality. Upon detecting malicious activity, an EDR system can take automated or manual action to contain the threat. This may include isolating the affected endpoint from the network to prevent lateral movement, killing malicious processes, quarantining files, or executing custom scripts to remediate system changes. In some cases, EDR solutions can roll back changes made by ransomware or other destructive malware using snapshot-based recovery features. These rapid response mechanisms are crucial in stopping threats before they can escalate and cause broader damage to the organization.

EDR also supports threat hunting, a proactive security practice where analysts search for hidden threats that may not have triggered alerts. Using the detailed telemetry collected from endpoints, threat hunters can query specific indicators, patterns, or behaviors across the entire environment. For example, they may look for evidence of persistence mechanisms, unusual privilege escalation attempts, or unauthorized use of administrative tools like PowerShell. By uncovering stealthy or dormant threats, threat hunting adds another layer of defense and improves the overall maturity of an organization's security operations.

Integration with other security tools is another important feature of EDR platforms. EDR can feed data into security information and event management (SIEM) systems for centralized correlation with logs from firewalls, identity systems, and cloud platforms. It can also work in conjunction with security orchestration, automation, and response (SOAR) tools to trigger automated incident workflows, notifications, and ticket creation. These integrations enhance situational awareness, improve response efficiency, and enable a coordinated defense strategy across multiple layers of the environment. Many EDR platforms also incorporate threat intelligence feeds to enrich alerts with information about known malware families, adversary tactics, and command-

and-control infrastructure. EDR solutions are designed with scalability in mind, capable of monitoring thousands of endpoints across diverse operating systems and geographic locations. Cloud-native EDR platforms offer centralized management and analytics, enabling organizations to manage policies, deploy agents, and investigate threats from a single interface. This is especially valuable in modern enterprises where endpoints are distributed across on-premises environments, remote workforces, and multi-cloud infrastructures. Policy enforcement, agent health monitoring, and software updates can all be managed remotely, reducing the administrative burden on IT and security teams.

In a threat landscape where attackers use advanced techniques such as fileless malware, living-off-the-land binaries (LOLBins), and credential abuse, EDR provides the visibility and tools necessary to detect and disrupt attacks that would otherwise go unnoticed. Its continuous monitoring and historical data retention enable security teams to trace the entire lifecycle of an attack, from initial entry to post-compromise activities, and to apply those insights to strengthen defenses moving forward.

Chapter 8: Mobile and Remote Workforce Security

Mobile and remote workforce security has become a top priority for organizations as employees increasingly access corporate resources from locations outside the traditional office environment using a wide array of devices, networks, and applications. This shift, accelerated by global events and the rise of hybrid work models, has redefined the security perimeter, which now extends to every endpoint, connection, and user behavior. Securing a mobile and remote workforce requires a combination of technology, policy, and user awareness to manage risks that arise from distributed access, untrusted networks, personal devices, and varying levels of physical and digital control. One of the foundational elements of remote workforce security is ensuring secure access to corporate resources, which is typically achieved through the use of Virtual Private Networks (VPNs), Secure Access Service Edge (SASE) solutions, and Zero Trust Network Access (ZTNA) models. VPNs provide encrypted tunnels for remote connections but can be limited in scalability and visibility, while ZTNA solutions offer a more granular approach by authenticating users continuously and granting access only to the specific resources required.

Identity and access management plays a crucial role in securing mobile workers, as traditional device or network-based trust models are no longer sufficient. Strong user authentication, particularly through multi-factor authentication (MFA), helps ensure that access requests are legitimate even when initiated from unmanaged or unfamiliar environments. Conditional access policies further strengthen this model by evaluating the user's device compliance status, geolocation, login behavior, and other contextual signals before granting access. These policies allow organizations to block or limit access from high-risk scenarios, such as logins from unknown devices or locations known for cybercrime. Centralized identity platforms such as Azure AD or Okta help enforce these controls across multiple applications and services, providing consistent protection regardless of where users are connecting from.

Device security is another critical consideration, especially given the wide variety of endpoints used by remote employees. These devices may include corporate-issued laptops, personal smartphones, or even unmanaged tablets, each presenting unique security challenges. Mobile Device Management (MDM) and Mobile Application Management (MAM) solutions allow organizations to enforce security policies on mobile and remote endpoints, including encryption, password requirements, screen lock enforcement, remote wipe capabilities, and application restrictions. MAM solutions in particular are useful for BYOD environments, as they apply protections at the application level without controlling the entire device. Remote endpoint protection platforms should also include antivirus, firewall, and intrusion prevention features, along with integration into centralized monitoring and response tools to detect suspicious behavior across the fleet.

Data protection for remote and mobile users requires controls that secure data at rest, in transit, and in use. Full disk encryption ensures that data stored locally on a device remains protected in case of theft or loss, while secure file-sharing tools and encrypted communication channels protect data in motion. Cloud-based storage and collaboration platforms, such as Microsoft OneDrive or Google Workspace, should be configured with strict sharing policies, version control, and activity monitoring to prevent accidental or intentional data leakage. Data Loss Prevention (DLP) policies further reinforce these protections by inspecting outbound communications for sensitive data patterns and blocking or flagging violations in real time.

Monitoring and visibility into remote activities are essential for identifying threats and enforcing compliance. Endpoint Detection and Response (EDR) solutions deployed on remote devices collect telemetry data, detect anomalies, and enable centralized investigations. These tools help security teams understand if a device is behaving abnormally, accessing unauthorized resources, or exhibiting signs of compromise. Cloud Access Security Brokers (CASBs) add visibility into cloud application usage, allowing organizations to detect shadow IT, enforce access controls, and monitor data transfers across sanctioned and unsanctioned applications. Together, these solutions ensure that even devices operating outside the corporate network are monitored, protected, and governed according to organizational policies.

Security awareness training remains a key pillar of mobile workforce security, as users must understand how to recognize phishing attempts, avoid unsafe public Wi-Fi, use secure passwords, and report suspicious behavior. Regular simulated phishing tests, clear communication on new threats, and accessible support channels empower users to take ownership of their digital safety and contribute to the organization's overall resilience. A strong mobile and remote workforce security strategy is built on layered defenses, continuous monitoring, and user engagement, designed to adapt to the evolving ways people work while maintaining control over sensitive systems and data.

Chapter 9: Automation, AI, and Endpoint Threat Intelligence

Automation, AI, and endpoint threat intelligence have become critical components in the modern cybersecurity landscape, offering organizations the ability to detect, analyze, and respond to threats faster and more effectively than ever before. As threats evolve in complexity and speed, traditional manual approaches to endpoint security are no longer sufficient to keep pace with the volume of data, the sophistication of attacks, and the sheer number of endpoints across modern infrastructures. Automation reduces human error, eliminates repetitive tasks, and enables real-time enforcement of security policies across thousands of devices, while artificial intelligence and machine learning provide the intelligence layer necessary to identify unknown or emerging threats based on patterns and behavior rather than static signatures.

Automation in endpoint security is primarily driven by policy enforcement, event response, and system configuration. Security automation tools can be used to enforce compliance by ensuring devices meet baseline configurations, such as enforcing encryption, disabling unused services, and applying required patches. When an endpoint deviates from policy, automation tools can immediately trigger remediation actions like applying a patch, revoking access, or isolating the device from the network. In incident response, automation plays a vital role by executing predefined playbooks that include steps like quarantining a device, collecting forensic data, alerting analysts, and integrating with ticketing systems. These actions, which once required manual intervention, can now occur within seconds of detection, significantly reducing the window of opportunity for attackers to inflict damage.

Artificial intelligence enhances endpoint security by analyzing massive volumes of endpoint data to identify anomalies and suspicious behavior that may indicate a threat. AI-driven security platforms ingest and analyze data from logs, user activity, file changes, process behavior, and network connections, building baselines of normal activity and flagging deviations in real time. Unlike traditional rules-based systems that rely on known indicators of compromise, AI models learn from past data to recognize the subtle signs of novel attacks. This capability is particularly valuable in detecting zero-day threats, fileless malware, and insider attacks that may not trigger signature-based alerts. Machine learning algorithms continuously improve over time, refining their detection capabilities and reducing false positives as they are exposed to more data and analyst feedback.

Endpoint threat intelligence brings contextual awareness to detection and response efforts by enriching endpoint data with external insights into attacker tools, tactics, and infrastructure. Threat intelligence can include indicators such as known malicious IP addresses, file hashes, domain names, or URLs, as well as behavioral patterns associated with specific threat actors. By correlating endpoint activity with threat intelligence feeds, security platforms can prioritize alerts, recognize attack campaigns, and determine the likely intent behind suspicious behavior. For example, if an endpoint connects to a domain known to be associated with a command-and-control server, that behavior can be immediately flagged as high risk, triggering a response workflow based on the severity and relevance of the threat.

The combination of automation, AI, and threat intelligence creates a synergistic effect, where detection becomes faster, response becomes more precise, and context becomes richer. Security teams can focus their efforts on high-priority incidents while relying on automated systems to handle routine analysis and response tasks. In some environments, AI-driven endpoint detection and response (EDR) platforms are capable of autonomously remediating threats, documenting actions taken, and presenting analysts with clear summaries of the event. These platforms often integrate with security information and event management (SIEM) and security orchestration, automation, and response (SOAR) systems to facilitate end-to-end visibility and coordinated incident handling.

Automated threat hunting is another powerful application of these technologies, where AI continuously scans endpoint data for patterns or relationships that suggest compromise, without waiting for alerts to be generated. This proactive capability helps identify threats that are stealthy or dormant, improving the organization's ability to detect and mitigate risks early in the attack lifecycle. In a world where endpoints are distributed, mobile, and constantly connected, the combination of automation, artificial intelligence, and actionable threat intelligence is essential to maintaining a security posture that is both responsive and adaptive to change.

Chapter 10: Incident Response at the Endpoint Level

Incident response at the endpoint level is a critical function within a modern cybersecurity strategy, focusing on detecting, containing, investigating, and remediating security incidents that originate or manifest on endpoint devices. These devices, which include laptops, desktops, servers, and mobile platforms, represent the frontline of organizational security and are often the first targets in cyberattacks. When an incident occurs at the endpoint—whether it's a malware infection, ransomware attack, privilege escalation, or unauthorized access attempt—the speed and precision of the response determine how effectively the threat can be neutralized and how much damage can be prevented. Incident response at this level begins with visibility, which is provided by endpoint detection and response (EDR) platforms, security agents, and logging tools that continuously monitor processes, user activity, file changes, registry modifications, and network connections in real time.

Once suspicious activity is detected, the next step is to accurately assess and classify the event. This involves correlating observed behavior with known indicators of compromise, threat intelligence, and contextual information about the affected system. For example, an unusual child process spawned by a Microsoft Office document, combined with a network connection to a rare domain, may be flagged as indicative of a phishing-based malware infection. Analysts must determine whether the event is benign, suspicious, or malicious, and this triage process relies heavily on detailed endpoint telemetry and behavioral baselines. EDR platforms often provide visual tools such as process trees and attack timelines to aid in this investigation, allowing responders to understand how the incident began, what actions were taken, and whether other endpoints may be affected.

Containment is the next priority in endpoint-level incident response and is designed to prevent the threat from spreading across the environment. This might involve isolating the affected device from the network, stopping a specific process, or blocking communication with external servers. Automated response actions are particularly valuable in this phase, as they reduce response time and minimize reliance on manual intervention. For instance, a compromised endpoint identified as part of a ransomware attack can be automatically disconnected from the corporate network and placed into a quarantine state, halting the attacker's ability to encrypt additional systems or exfiltrate data. These actions must be carefully logged and managed to ensure they do not interfere with evidence preservation or incident documentation.

After containment, the focus shifts to eradication and recovery. Eradication involves removing the malicious artifacts from the endpoint, which could include deleting malicious files, uninstalling rogue software, killing malicious processes, and restoring altered configurations. In cases where the system has been deeply compromised, a full reimage or system rebuild may be necessary. Recovery involves restoring the endpoint to a trusted operational state, which includes verifying system integrity, reapplying hardening policies, and ensuring that all patches and updates are current. During this stage, it's important to monitor the device for any signs of reinfection or residual malicious activity, particularly in environments where the initial infection vector may still be present, such as an undetected phishing campaign or vulnerable remote desktop service.

Documentation and post-incident analysis are essential parts of endpoint incident response. Every step taken during the response—from initial detection to final remediation—must be recorded in detail to support compliance requirements, improve future response efforts, and inform broader risk management strategies. Analysts conduct a postmortem to understand what enabled the attack, how effective the response was, and what improvements can be made to detection, response times, or preventive controls. These lessons are then used to update incident response playbooks, refine alerting mechanisms, and enhance security awareness training.

Threat containment at the endpoint is not an isolated effort but is part of a larger incident response process that often involves coordination with network, identity, and cloud teams. Information gathered from the endpoint investigation may indicate broader compromise, such as credential theft, lateral movement, or the presence of persistence mechanisms across multiple systems. Integration with SIEM and SOAR platforms allows endpoint-level insights to trigger enterprise-wide actions, such as updating firewall rules, blocking attacker infrastructure, or launching a coordinated hunt across all systems. By focusing on fast, intelligent, and well-documented response at the endpoint, organizations can significantly reduce the impact of security incidents and build a more resilient overall security posture.

BOOK 3
DEFENDING THE CLOUD PERIMETER
BEST PRACTICES FOR CLOUD-BASED NETWORK SECURITY

ROB BOTWRIGHT

Chapter 1: Rethinking the Perimeter in the Cloud Era

Rethinking the perimeter in the cloud era represents a fundamental shift away from traditional security models that relied on clearly defined network boundaries and centralized protection. In the past, the network perimeter was straightforward—organizations placed their valuable resources behind firewalls and assumed that anything within that boundary was safe, while external connections were treated as inherently risky. Today, the widespread adoption of cloud computing, remote work, mobile devices, and interconnected applications has blurred these once-distinct boundaries, making it increasingly difficult to define where an organization's security perimeter begins or ends. The perimeter now extends across public cloud platforms, hybrid environments, third-party services, and even personal devices used for corporate activities. This evolution requires security teams to reconsider the very concept of a perimeter, recognizing that traditional network-based defenses alone are inadequate for protecting assets in dynamic, distributed environments.

Cloud computing has dramatically expanded the attack surface by placing sensitive data and critical workloads outside traditional data centers, often in environments managed by third-party cloud providers. Organizations using services such as AWS, Azure, or Google Cloud must understand that security is a shared responsibility, with providers securing the infrastructure itself, while customers remain responsible for securing their data, applications, and configurations. This shared model means security teams can no longer rely on physical control or direct oversight of hardware and network infrastructure. Instead, they must rely on cloud-native security controls, such as virtual firewalls, identity-based access management, encryption, and comprehensive monitoring to protect their data and applications.

Identity has become the new security perimeter in the cloud era, as traditional network-centric protections lose effectiveness in environments where users, applications, and data reside outside organizational networks. Instead of focusing solely on physical or logical locations, security now emphasizes verifying identities and controlling access based on roles, permissions, device health, user behavior, and real-time contextual signals. Zero Trust architectures, which operate on the principle of "never trust, always verify," reflect this shift by requiring continuous validation of identities and devices, regardless of their location or network affiliation. Identity providers and Single Sign-On

(SSO) services are central to this approach, allowing organizations to enforce strong authentication measures, apply multi-factor authentication (MFA), and dynamically evaluate user risk based on behavior, location, and device posture.

Microsegmentation has emerged as a key technique for rethinking the perimeter in cloud and hybrid environments. Rather than defining broad network segments with coarse security policies, microsegmentation applies granular security controls at the workload, application, or service level. This means that each resource or group of resources can have specific access policies that restrict traffic based on identities, workloads, and contextual information, dramatically limiting the ability of attackers to move laterally within the environment. Technologies such as software-defined networking (SDN) and container orchestration tools like Kubernetes enable organizations to implement microsegmentation dynamically and at scale, providing detailed visibility and control over network flows, regardless of whether resources are hosted on-premises, in the cloud, or across multi-cloud environments.

Cloud access security brokers (CASBs) and secure access service edge (SASE) architectures have also played pivotal roles in redefining perimeter security for cloud-centric organizations. CASBs provide visibility, control, and threat protection for data and applications hosted in cloud services, enabling organizations to enforce consistent security policies and compliance controls across multiple SaaS providers. SASE combines wide-area networking with cloud-native security functions such as firewall as a service (FWaaS), Zero Trust Network Access (ZTNA), and secure web gateways, delivering security directly at the edge, close to users and their applications. This approach ensures security controls are consistently applied, regardless of the user's location or the specific cloud or data center they are accessing.

Visibility and monitoring become even more essential as the perimeter expands and dissolves into distributed cloud and edge environments. Comprehensive logging, event correlation, and continuous monitoring are required to detect threats and anomalous activities across these dispersed resources. Cloud-native monitoring tools integrated with Security Information and Event Management (SIEM) platforms enable organizations to track user behavior, application usage, and configuration changes in real-time, quickly identifying suspicious activities or misconfigurations before they can be exploited. Automation and artificial intelligence enhance these capabilities, allowing security teams to detect threats proactively and respond rapidly across the entire extended perimeter.

As organizations continue to evolve their use of cloud and hybrid infrastructure, the perimeter will further shift towards identity-driven, application-specific, and context-aware security approaches. Organizations that recognize and adapt to this new reality will position themselves to securely leverage cloud innovations, maintaining visibility, control, and protection despite the ongoing challenges posed by increasingly fluid and dynamic digital environments.

Chapter 2: Shared Responsibility and Cloud Security Models

Shared responsibility and cloud security models form the foundational framework for understanding how security is managed in cloud computing environments, where both cloud service providers and customers share distinct obligations for protecting data, systems, and services. This model clearly defines which components of the infrastructure are secured by the provider and which remain the responsibility of the customer, ensuring that both parties understand their roles and avoid security gaps that could arise from misconfiguration or assumption. In Infrastructure as a Service (IaaS), for example, the cloud provider is typically responsible for securing the underlying physical infrastructure, including data centers, networking hardware, hypervisors, and physical storage, while the customer is responsible for configuring and securing the operating systems, applications, identity and access controls, and data stored or processed within the virtual machines.

In Platform as a Service (PaaS), the provider's responsibility expands to include securing the platform layer itself, such as databases, runtime environments, and development frameworks, leaving the customer responsible for application code, data, and user access. Software as a Service (SaaS) shifts even more responsibility to the provider, who manages the application, infrastructure, and platform components, while customers are generally responsible for user access, data classification, and endpoint security. Each cloud model reduces operational burden for the customer to varying degrees, but none of them absolve the customer of security responsibilities entirely. Misunderstanding where the provider's responsibility ends and the customer's begins is one of the most common causes of cloud-related security incidents.

Misconfigurations, such as public storage buckets, overly permissive access controls, and exposed APIs, often arise because organizations incorrectly assume that cloud providers will secure everything. While providers offer powerful tools and services for security, it is up to the customer to configure them appropriately. Cloud providers typically supply built-in features such as identity and access management (IAM), encryption options, firewall rules, and monitoring capabilities, but they do not automatically activate or configure these features to align with an organization's specific needs. Customers must actively manage these controls to enforce least privilege, enable logging, implement key management, and monitor usage to detect anomalies or abuse.

Compliance is another aspect influenced by the shared responsibility model. While cloud providers often meet regulatory requirements for the infrastructure they manage, customers must still ensure that their use of the cloud adheres to industry regulations, such as GDPR, HIPAA, or PCI DSS. This involves understanding how data is stored, processed, and accessed, and implementing controls to protect it accordingly. Encryption of data at rest and in transit, logging of access events, regular auditing, and privacy impact assessments are all measures that fall under the customer's domain. The shared responsibility model is not static; it may shift slightly based on the services in use or the configurations chosen by the customer.

Cloud security models also emphasize the need for collaboration between security teams, cloud architects, and compliance officers to ensure that security policies are aligned with cloud capabilities and that controls are continuously monitored and updated. Automation tools, such as infrastructure as code, can help enforce secure configurations consistently across deployments, while security posture management solutions provide visibility into misconfigurations and compliance drift. Understanding and properly implementing the shared responsibility model is essential for organizations to build secure and resilient cloud environments, enabling them to take advantage of cloud innovation while maintaining control over their security obligations.

Chapter 3: Securing IaaS, PaaS, and SaaS Environments

Securing IaaS, PaaS, and SaaS environments requires a tailored approach that reflects the unique risks, responsibilities, and architectural characteristics of each cloud service model. In Infrastructure as a Service (IaaS), customers are given the highest level of control and flexibility, but with that control comes a greater burden for security management. IaaS environments provide access to virtualized computing resources such as virtual machines, storage, and networking components, and it is the responsibility of the customer to secure the operating systems, applications, data, identity management, and network configurations deployed on top of the infrastructure. Misconfigurations in IaaS environments—such as publicly exposed storage containers, unrestricted network security groups, or default administrative credentials—are among the most common causes of data breaches. Implementing network segmentation, deploying host-based firewalls, enforcing strict access control policies, and using automation tools to apply consistent security configurations are foundational practices in securing IaaS environments. Logging and monitoring using services such as AWS CloudTrail or Azure Monitor provide essential visibility into activity across the environment and should be configured to generate alerts for suspicious behavior.

In PaaS environments, the cloud provider manages the underlying infrastructure, runtime, and development tools, while the customer is responsible for the security of the applications they build and the data they process. Securing PaaS begins with ensuring that secure coding practices are followed, input validation is enforced, and applications are scanned for vulnerabilities before deployment. Identity and access management becomes even more critical, as developers and applications interact with various services through APIs and credentials. Secrets management tools such as AWS Secrets Manager or Azure Key Vault should be used to store API keys, database passwords, and other sensitive information securely. Additionally, PaaS services often include managed databases, containers, and functions, all of which require security hardening. For example, configuring database services to use encryption at rest and in transit, enabling automatic backups, and restricting access to only authorized IP addresses or service identities are important steps in reducing risk. Event-driven compute services such as serverless functions must be tightly scoped with permissions and monitored for excessive invocation, which could indicate abuse or exploitation.

Securing Software as a Service (SaaS) environments involves a different set of priorities because customers have limited control over the application and infrastructure. The responsibility in SaaS lies primarily in configuring security settings, managing user access, protecting data, and ensuring compliance with organizational policies. Common SaaS platforms such as Microsoft 365, Google Workspace, and Salesforce offer a range of security features, including multi-factor authentication (MFA), data loss prevention (DLP), role-based access control, and activity logging. Ensuring these features are properly enabled and configured is key to reducing risk. Additionally, SaaS environments must be continuously monitored for suspicious login activity, configuration drift, and unauthorized data sharing. Integrating SaaS platforms with identity providers through SSO and centralized directory services helps streamline user access management and enforce consistent authentication policies. SaaS security posture management (SSPM) solutions can be used to audit SaaS configurations, monitor compliance with security policies, and detect anomalies in usage patterns across multiple services.

Across all three models— IaaS, PaaS, and SaaS— data protection remains a central theme. Data must be classified according to sensitivity and protected accordingly through encryption, access controls, and regular auditing. Organizations must ensure that data residency and compliance requirements are met by configuring storage locations and retention policies within the cloud platforms. Logging and monitoring should be implemented consistently, and alerts should be integrated into centralized security operations platforms such as SIEM or SOAR to allow timely investigation and response. Secure API usage is another cross-cutting concern, especially as cloud applications increasingly rely on third-party integrations and machine-to-machine communication. API access should be authenticated using strong mechanisms such as OAuth, access should be limited by scopes or roles, and usage should be monitored for unusual activity.

Governance and policy enforcement also span all three service models, requiring clear documentation of security roles, incident response plans, and acceptable use policies. Security automation and infrastructure as code can help enforce baseline configurations and detect drift over time, reducing manual overhead and ensuring consistency across deployments. Security must be built into the entire lifecycle of cloud adoption, from planning and provisioning to operations and decommissioning, with continuous risk assessment guiding improvements in strategy and technology.

Chapter 4: Cloud Firewalls and Virtual Network Appliances

Cloud firewalls and virtual network appliances play a central role in securing cloud-based infrastructure by controlling traffic flow, enforcing access policies, and inspecting data in transit across virtual networks. As organizations move workloads to public and hybrid cloud environments, the traditional concept of perimeter-based firewalls becomes less effective due to the dynamic and decentralized nature of cloud architectures. In this context, cloud firewalls and virtual appliances are used to provide the same foundational protections found in physical data centers, but with the scalability, flexibility, and automation necessary for cloud-native environments. Cloud firewalls are typically offered as a service by cloud providers and integrate directly with virtual networks, enabling granular control over inbound and outbound traffic at the subnet or instance level. These cloud-native firewalls can be configured through provider-specific tools such as AWS Network Firewall, Azure Firewall, or Google Cloud Firewall, which allow administrators to define rule sets, apply security policies to virtual machines, and monitor traffic flows through centralized dashboards.

Unlike traditional firewalls that rely on static rules and physical interfaces, cloud firewalls are designed to operate in dynamic environments where resources are constantly changing. They can automatically adapt to new instances being spun up, services being scaled, or IP ranges being modified, ensuring that security controls remain effective as the infrastructure evolves. Rules can be applied based on IP addresses, ports, protocols, tags, or security groups, providing flexibility in how policies are enforced across workloads. For example, traffic between web servers and application servers can be restricted to specific ports and protocols, while traffic from the internet can be limited to only certain public-facing endpoints. Logging and alerting capabilities are built into these services, allowing security teams to detect unauthorized access attempts, misconfigurations, or other anomalies in real time.

Virtual network appliances extend the capabilities of cloud-native firewalls by offering advanced security functions typically provided by traditional hardware-based devices, now delivered as virtualized software. These appliances include next-generation firewalls (NGFW), intrusion prevention systems (IPS), deep packet inspection, and secure web gateways, all of which can be deployed within a cloud environment as virtual machines or containers. Vendors such as Palo Alto Networks, Fortinet, and Check Point provide virtual appliances that integrate with cloud orchestration tools, offering centralized policy management, threat intelligence feeds, and automated response capabilities. These solutions are particularly valuable in hybrid environments or for organizations that need consistent security across on-premises and cloud infrastructure.

Deploying virtual appliances in the cloud involves careful consideration of network topology, performance requirements, and fault tolerance. Appliances are typically inserted into the traffic path between subnets, virtual private networks (VPNs), or cloud gateways, where they can inspect and control traffic at the application layer. High availability can be achieved by deploying multiple instances across availability zones, using load balancers and health checks to ensure failover and continuous protection. Scalability is managed through auto-scaling groups, allowing virtual appliances to increase or decrease in number based on traffic volume and performance thresholds. Cost management is also important, as virtual appliances consume compute and storage resources, and organizations must balance security requirements with operational efficiency.

Cloud firewalls and virtual appliances also support microsegmentation by allowing traffic controls to be applied between workloads within the same virtual network. This approach limits lateral movement by attackers and ensures that compromise of one service does not lead to uncontrolled access to others. Security policies can be enforced at the virtual network interface level, enabling organizations to implement Zero Trust principles by verifying and restricting traffic between every component of an application or service. Additionally, integration with identity and access management systems allows policies to be applied based on user or service identity, adding another layer of contextual control.

Both cloud firewalls and virtual appliances contribute to compliance by enabling organizations to demonstrate control over traffic flows, enforce data sovereignty, and generate detailed audit logs. These controls can be mapped to industry standards such as PCI DSS, HIPAA, or

ISO 27001, and integrated with centralized security operations for continuous monitoring. As cloud environments become more complex and interconnected, cloud firewalls and virtual network appliances provide the visibility, control, and enforcement mechanisms needed to secure critical assets and maintain operational integrity.

Chapter 5: Identity and Access Management in the Cloud

Identity and Access Management in the cloud is one of the most critical pillars of cloud security, acting as the foundation for ensuring that the right individuals and services have appropriate access to the right resources at the right time. Unlike traditional on-premises environments where access was often controlled through centralized directory services and internal network boundaries, cloud environments are dynamic, decentralized, and designed for accessibility across geographies, platforms, and devices. This shift makes it essential to rethink how identities are managed and how access is granted, monitored, and revoked in a scalable and secure way. In cloud environments, identities can belong to users, services, applications, or even machines, each of which may require different levels of access and operate under different contextual conditions. Managing these identities effectively requires the use of cloud-native IAM tools, federated identity systems, and policy-driven access models that adapt to the needs of modern cloud usage.

Cloud providers such as AWS, Azure, and Google Cloud offer built-in IAM services that allow organizations to create and manage identities, define roles and permissions, and control access to cloud resources at a granular level. These services enable administrators to follow the principle of least privilege, ensuring that users and services are only granted the minimum access necessary to perform their functions. Role-based access control (RBAC) is a common approach used in these environments, where predefined roles are associated with specific sets of permissions, and users are assigned roles based on their job function. In more advanced scenarios, attribute-based access control (ABAC) is used, where access decisions are based on a combination of user attributes, resource attributes, and environmental conditions such as time of day or network location. This allows for greater flexibility and context-aware access control policies.

Single sign-on (SSO) and identity federation are essential for managing access across multiple cloud platforms and Software as a Service (SaaS) applications. By integrating with identity providers such as Azure Active Directory, Okta, or Ping Identity, organizations can centralize authentication, reduce the number of credentials users must manage, and enforce consistent access policies across environments. Federated identity also allows organizations to extend their existing identity infrastructure to cloud platforms, enabling seamless access without duplicating identity data or maintaining multiple authentication systems. This integration enhances security by enabling unified policy enforcement, multi-factor authentication (MFA), and centralized audit logging.

Multi-factor authentication is a non-negotiable component of cloud IAM, as it dramatically reduces the risk of account compromise due to stolen or weak credentials. MFA requires users to provide two or more forms of verification, such as a password and a one-time code sent to a trusted device, before access is granted. Modern implementations also support biometric factors, hardware tokens, or authentication apps that provide push notifications or time-based codes. Enforcing MFA across all privileged accounts and sensitive resources adds a critical layer of security and should be enforced by default in all cloud environments.

Another vital aspect of cloud IAM is lifecycle management, which ensures that identities are properly created, modified, and deactivated in accordance with role changes, onboarding, or offboarding processes. Failure to properly manage identity lifecycles can result in orphaned accounts, excessive privileges, and unnecessary exposure of sensitive resources. Automated provisioning and deprovisioning processes, often integrated with human resources systems or identity governance tools, help maintain clean, accurate, and compliant identity data. Privileged access management (PAM) adds further controls by limiting administrative access through just-in-time elevation, session recording, and credential vaulting, reducing the risk of insider threats or credential misuse.

Auditing and monitoring are critical to ensuring the effectiveness of IAM policies in the cloud. All access events, including login attempts, permission changes, and resource access, should be logged and reviewed regularly. Cloud providers offer native logging services such as AWS CloudTrail, Azure AD logs, and Google Cloud Audit Logs, which can be integrated into SIEM platforms for real-time analysis and alerting. These logs provide visibility into who accessed what, when, and from where, allowing security teams to detect anomalies, investigate incidents, and demonstrate compliance with regulatory requirements. As cloud adoption continues to grow, robust identity and access management remains central to protecting cloud assets, preventing unauthorized access, and enabling secure digital transformation.

Chapter 6: Cloud Access Security Brokers (CASBs)

Cloud Access Security Brokers (CASBs) are a critical component in modern cloud security strategies, serving as control points that sit between cloud service consumers and cloud service providers to enforce security policies, monitor activity, and ensure compliance. As organizations increasingly adopt cloud-based services such as Software as a Service (SaaS), Platform as a Service (PaaS), and Infrastructure as a Service (IaaS), the need for visibility and control over how data is accessed, shared, and stored in these environments becomes paramount. CASBs bridge the gap between traditional security controls and the decentralized nature of the cloud, providing organizations with the ability to monitor user behavior, control data movement, detect threats, and ensure that cloud usage aligns with internal policies and regulatory requirements.

One of the primary functions of a CASB is to deliver visibility into sanctioned and unsanctioned cloud application usage across the organization. Employees often use unsanctioned cloud services, known as shadow IT, without the knowledge or approval of the IT or security departments. This creates significant blind spots where sensitive data may be uploaded, shared, or stored in unmanaged environments, exposing the organization to data leakage or regulatory violations. CASBs can discover all cloud applications in use by analyzing network traffic, browser activity, or API integrations, providing a comprehensive inventory of cloud usage and enabling security teams to assess the associated risks. Once identified, organizations can classify applications as sanctioned or unsanctioned and apply appropriate controls to restrict or monitor access.

Another key capability of CASBs is enforcing data security policies across multiple cloud platforms. This includes applying encryption, tokenization, or redaction to sensitive information before it is uploaded to the cloud, ensuring that data remains protected regardless of the cloud provider's native security capabilities. CASBs also support Data Loss Prevention (DLP) by inspecting content in real time and preventing the unauthorized sharing or transmission of data that matches predefined patterns, such as credit card numbers, personal identifiers, or confidential documents. These controls help prevent accidental or intentional data exposure, particularly in SaaS environments where users often have the ability to share files publicly or with external collaborators.

CASBs also enhance threat protection by analyzing user behavior and detecting anomalies that may indicate compromised accounts, insider threats, or malicious activity. By establishing behavioral baselines and using machine learning algorithms, CASBs can identify unusual login patterns, excessive data downloads, or access from unfamiliar locations and devices. When such behavior is detected, CASBs can trigger automated responses, such as revoking access tokens, requiring multi-factor authentication, alerting administrators, or quarantining files. These capabilities extend the organization's security monitoring into the cloud and provide a layer of real-time defense that is essential for rapid incident detection and response.

Compliance management is another critical area where CASBs provide value. Organizations must comply with various regulatory frameworks such as GDPR, HIPAA, PCI DSS, and ISO 27001, which often include requirements for data residency, access control, audit logging, and breach notification. CASBs assist in meeting these obligations by offering tools to enforce policies across cloud applications, generate compliance reports, and maintain audit trails of user activity. With unified policy management, security teams can apply consistent controls across diverse cloud platforms, reducing complexity and ensuring that compliance requirements are met without hindering productivity.

Deployment models for CASBs include API-based integration, reverse proxy, forward proxy, and agent-based approaches, each with its advantages and limitations. API-based deployment offers seamless integration with cloud services and provides deep visibility into data and user actions without altering traffic flow, but it may have limited real-time enforcement capabilities. Proxy-based models offer more immediate control and inspection of traffic but can introduce latency or require configuration changes on user devices. Organizations often choose a hybrid deployment model to balance visibility, performance, and enforcement depending on the use case, application type, and risk tolerance.

By acting as a centralized control point for cloud service usage, CASBs empower organizations to safely adopt cloud services while maintaining security, visibility, and compliance. They allow security teams to extend traditional controls into the cloud, enforce policies consistently, and respond swiftly to emerging threats in an environment where users, data, and applications are more distributed than ever before.

Chapter 7: Securing APIs and Application Gateways

Securing APIs and application gateways is a vital part of modern cloud and web application security, as APIs are now the backbone of communication between services, applications, and systems across distributed environments. As organizations move toward microservices architectures, adopt serverless computing, and expose services to partners and third-party developers, APIs become both a powerful enabler and a significant point of risk. APIs provide structured, programmable access to backend systems, databases, and business logic, and if not properly secured, they can expose sensitive data, allow unauthorized access, or serve as entry points for a variety of attacks such as injection, data scraping, and privilege escalation. Application gateways, on the other hand, act as centralized entry points for managing and securing traffic into APIs and web applications, enforcing policies such as routing, load balancing, authentication, and threat protection.

The foundation of API security begins with authentication and authorization. APIs should never allow unauthenticated access unless they are explicitly intended to be public and even then, rate limiting and behavioral monitoring are recommended. OAuth 2.0 and OpenID Connect have become standard frameworks for securing APIs, enabling token-based authentication where clients request access tokens from an identity provider and present those tokens to access protected APIs. These tokens must be validated by the API gateway or backend service to ensure they are unexpired, unaltered, and issued by a trusted authority. Fine-grained authorization should be applied using scopes or roles defined within the token, restricting what each user or system is allowed to do with the API.

Input validation is another crucial defense mechanism for APIs. Since APIs process user input, failing to validate and sanitize input properly can lead to injection attacks, such as SQL injection, command injection, or XML external entity (XXE) attacks. All incoming data should be validated against strict schemas, rejected if it does not conform, and handled with care when passed to downstream systems. This also helps prevent accidental misuse of APIs and improves the reliability of services. Rate limiting and throttling are necessary to prevent abuse, denial-of-service attempts, and brute-force attacks. By limiting the number of API requests per minute or hour from a given IP address or token, services can protect themselves from being overwhelmed or exploited.

Application gateways provide centralized enforcement of security policies for APIs and web applications, allowing consistent control over authentication, authorization, traffic inspection, and request routing. These gateways, such as Azure Application Gateway, AWS API Gateway, or NGINX, act as reverse proxies, terminating incoming connections and applying rules before forwarding traffic to backend services. They can enforce SSL/TLS encryption, block or rate-limit malicious requests, rewrite URLs, inspect headers for suspicious patterns, and integrate with Web Application Firewalls (WAFs) for deeper inspection. When integrated with threat intelligence feeds and anomaly detection, application gateways can also recognize and mitigate attacks in real time based on known bad IP addresses or unusual request behavior.

API gateways also support versioning and access control at the API level, enabling the publication of different versions of an API to different audiences or stages of development. This allows for a gradual rollout of changes, minimizes the impact of deprecating older APIs, and provides developers with a controlled environment for testing. Role-based access and API keys can be used to restrict usage per developer, application, or partner, helping organizations maintain control over how their APIs are consumed. Logging and monitoring are critical for both APIs and application gateways. All access attempts, whether successful or not, should be logged with context such as IP address, user identity, request details, and response status. These logs should be centralized, retained securely, and analyzed to detect anomalies or signs of attack.

Automated tools such as API security scanners and static analysis platforms should be integrated into development pipelines to identify vulnerabilities early in the software development lifecycle. Secure design principles must be applied from the beginning, with security requirements defined alongside functional requirements. API documentation should be carefully managed and reviewed, as overly permissive or inaccurate documentation can lead to unintentional data exposure or misuse. By combining robust authentication, policy enforcement, input validation, threat detection, and secure design, organizations can ensure that their APIs and application gateways serve as secure and reliable interfaces in increasingly interconnected and cloud-native environments.

Chapter 8: Encryption and Key Management in Cloud Environments

Encryption and key management in cloud environments are essential components of a robust data protection strategy, especially as organizations increasingly store sensitive information in public, private, and hybrid cloud infrastructures. Encryption ensures that data remains confidential by transforming it into an unreadable format unless accessed by authorized entities with the correct cryptographic keys, while key management governs the generation, storage, distribution, rotation, and destruction of those keys. In the cloud, encryption must be applied comprehensively to data at rest, in transit, and, where feasible, in use, to protect against unauthorized access, data breaches, insider threats, and legal or regulatory exposure. Cloud providers offer built-in encryption services for storage, databases, file systems, and communication channels, but customers are responsible for configuring, managing, and validating these controls based on their specific security and compliance requirements.

Data at rest in cloud environments refers to information stored on disks, databases, object storage, or backup volumes. Most major cloud platforms provide native support for encrypting data at rest using either provider-managed keys or customer-managed keys. For example, AWS uses server-side encryption with services such as S3, EBS, and RDS, while Azure and Google Cloud offer similar capabilities through their respective encryption services. Server-side encryption ensures that data is encrypted before it is written to disk and decrypted automatically when accessed by an authorized user or service. Customers can choose to rely on the provider's default encryption keys or take control of the process by supplying their own keys through Key Management Services (KMS) or Hardware Security Modules (HSMs), which add an additional layer of trust, transparency, and accountability.

Data in transit includes any information moving between users and cloud services, or between internal services within a cloud architecture. Encrypting data in transit is essential to protect against man-in-the-middle attacks, packet sniffing, and session hijacking. Cloud providers enforce transport layer encryption using protocols such as HTTPS with TLS, ensuring secure connections between clients and services. For inter-service communication within cloud environments, organizations can implement mutual TLS (mTLS), VPN tunnels, or software-defined perimeters to ensure that only authenticated endpoints can communicate, and that data remains encrypted as it moves through internal networks. Secure configurations of APIs, databases, message queues, and load balancers must be validated to guarantee that all data is encrypted during transmission.

Data in use, though more complex to secure, refers to data that is actively being processed in memory. Traditional encryption methods typically decrypt data before processing, which creates a brief window of vulnerability. Emerging technologies such as homomorphic encryption, secure enclaves, and confidential computing aim to close this gap by allowing data to be processed while still encrypted or within protected memory regions. Though still in development or limited in scope, these technologies represent the next frontier of encryption in cloud environments, especially for sensitive or regulated workloads.

Key management is the backbone of any encryption strategy, as the strength of encryption depends on the secrecy and proper handling of the cryptographic keys. Cloud-native KMS solutions like AWS KMS, Azure Key Vault, and Google Cloud KMS allow organizations to manage encryption keys securely and integrate them with cloud services. These systems provide lifecycle management for keys, including automated rotation, granular access control through IAM policies, audit logging of key usage, and the ability to import or generate keys within FIPS-compliant HSMs. The separation of duties is a key principle in key management, where access to the keys and the data they protect is divided among different roles or systems to reduce risk.

Organizations must also establish policies for key rotation, expiration, and revocation. Regular key rotation limits the exposure of compromised keys and ensures compliance with regulatory requirements. Secure deletion of keys, especially those associated with deprecated workloads or expired data retention periods, is essential to prevent unauthorized data recovery. Logging and monitoring are integral to key management, providing visibility into who accessed a key, when, and for what purpose. These logs must be protected against tampering and integrated into centralized security information and event management systems for real-time alerting and forensic investigation.

In multi-cloud or hybrid environments, centralized key management becomes more complex, requiring interoperability between different cloud KMS platforms or the use of external key management systems. Bring Your Own Key (BYOK) and Hold Your Own Key (HYOK) models allow organizations to retain control over their encryption keys, often for legal or compliance reasons, while still using public cloud services. These models require careful planning, integration, and governance to maintain the confidentiality, integrity, and availability of encrypted data across diverse environments.

Chapter 9: Continuous Compliance and Cloud Governance

Continuous compliance and cloud governance are essential pillars in securing and managing cloud environments at scale, especially as organizations adopt increasingly complex multi-cloud and hybrid architectures. In contrast to traditional IT compliance models, which often rely on periodic audits and manual checklists, continuous compliance is a proactive and automated approach that ensures security controls, configurations, and policies are continuously enforced and validated against regulatory requirements and internal standards. This shift is necessary in cloud environments, where infrastructure is dynamic, services are provisioned and deprovisioned rapidly, and the margin for error is high due to the speed and scale of deployment. Cloud governance complements continuous compliance by providing the strategic framework that defines how cloud resources are used, who can access them, how costs are managed, and how risk is controlled across the organization.

At the core of continuous compliance is automation. Tools and platforms are configured to monitor cloud environments in real time, evaluate configurations against compliance benchmarks such as CIS benchmarks, NIST frameworks, or ISO 27001, and automatically alert or remediate deviations. Infrastructure as Code (IaC) plays a significant role in enabling this model by ensuring that resources are deployed in a standardized and compliant manner from the outset. By defining infrastructure using code, organizations can embed compliance rules directly into the deployment process, preventing non-compliant configurations from ever reaching production. Policy-as-Code further extends this capability, allowing compliance checks and governance policies to be codified and enforced during CI/CD pipelines and runtime operations using tools such as Open Policy Agent (OPA), HashiCorp Sentinel, or AWS Config rules.

Cloud governance begins with the establishment of clear policies regarding identity and access management, data protection, cost control, resource tagging, and workload classification. Organizations must define who has access to what resources, under which conditions, and with what privileges. Role-based access control (RBAC), attribute-based access control (ABAC), and just-in-time access provisioning are used to enforce least privilege and reduce the risk of excessive entitlements. Automated guardrails ensure that access policies are applied consistently across accounts, subscriptions, and services. Cloud providers offer native governance tools such as

AWS Organizations, Azure Policy, and Google Cloud Organization Policy Service, which help enforce management boundaries, apply service restrictions, and ensure adherence to organizational standards.

Resource tagging is another key element of governance that supports visibility, accountability, and cost management. Tags can include metadata such as owner, department, environment, data sensitivity, and compliance classification, and they enable organizations to filter, group, and manage resources based on business context. Enforcing mandatory tagging through automation ensures that every resource is traceable, which is crucial for security audits, budgeting, and operational oversight. In multi-account or multi-subscription environments, tagging policies allow centralized teams to monitor usage patterns, identify anomalies, and allocate costs accurately across business units.

Continuous compliance also depends on real-time monitoring, logging, and auditability. Security information and event management (SIEM) systems, cloud-native logging services, and compliance dashboards aggregate and correlate logs from cloud providers, network components, and endpoint agents to detect misconfigurations, unauthorized access, or policy violations. These platforms provide continuous insight into compliance status, generate alerts when controls drift from baselines, and produce detailed reports that can be used for internal governance or regulatory submission. Integrations with ticketing systems and SOAR platforms enable automated workflows that assign issues to appropriate teams and track resolution, helping to close the loop between detection and remediation.

Cost governance is another critical aspect of cloud governance. Without proper controls, cloud expenses can quickly escalate due to overprovisioning, orphaned resources, or inefficient workloads. Budgets, quotas, and alerts must be implemented to prevent financial waste, and spend analysis tools can provide visibility into usage trends and opportunities for optimization. Automated policies can shut down unused resources, resize instances based on performance metrics, or move data to lower-cost storage tiers. Cost governance is deeply interconnected with security and compliance, as financial mismanagement can often be a sign of resource sprawl, shadow IT, or ungoverned workloads that fall outside organizational oversight.

A mature cloud governance model also includes clear documentation, defined roles and responsibilities, and regular policy reviews. Governance boards, risk committees, or cross-functional teams should oversee cloud initiatives, review exception requests, and evaluate the impact of new technologies or regulatory changes. Continuous training and awareness programs ensure that developers, security teams, and operations staff understand their responsibilities and the tools available to help them stay compliant. By embedding governance and compliance into every stage of the cloud lifecycle—from planning and provisioning to operations and decommissioning—organizations can maintain a strong security posture, reduce risk, and confidently operate in fast-paced, cloud-native environments.

Chapter 10: Multi-Cloud and Hybrid Cloud Security Strategies

Multi-cloud and hybrid cloud security strategies are essential for organizations that distribute workloads across multiple cloud providers or combine on-premises infrastructure with cloud-based services. As enterprises increasingly adopt diverse cloud platforms to avoid vendor lock-in, optimize performance, reduce latency, or meet compliance requirements, security teams must contend with fragmented environments that lack unified visibility and control. Multi-cloud environments introduce complexity because each provider—whether it is AWS, Azure, Google Cloud, or others—has its own security controls, identity systems, policy frameworks, and logging formats. In hybrid cloud scenarios, where legacy systems coexist with scalable cloud infrastructure, organizations must bridge the gap between traditional perimeter-based security models and modern cloud-native security paradigms. This demands a holistic and coordinated approach that can consistently enforce policies, monitor activities, and respond to threats across all environments without creating blind spots or operational inefficiencies.

One of the most important aspects of multi-cloud and hybrid security is centralized identity and access management. Instead of managing separate identities and permissions across each platform, organizations should integrate cloud services with a central identity provider using standards such as SAML, OAuth, or OpenID Connect. Solutions like Azure Active Directory, Okta, or Ping Identity can be used to federate identities across multiple clouds and on-prem environments, enabling single sign-on (SSO), multi-factor authentication (MFA), and unified access policies. Enforcing least privilege through role-based access control (RBAC) or attribute-based access control (ABAC) is critical to reduce the risk of overprivileged accounts and limit the blast radius in the event of a compromise. Just-in-time access and time-bound permissions add further granularity, ensuring that elevated privileges are only granted when needed and revoked automatically afterward.

Visibility is a major challenge in distributed cloud architectures, and effective strategies must include tools that aggregate logs, metrics, and events from all environments into a centralized security information and event management (SIEM) platform. This allows for unified threat detection, incident correlation, and compliance reporting. Cloud-native services like AWS CloudTrail, Azure

Monitor, and Google Cloud Audit Logs should be integrated into a centralized logging infrastructure, enriched with context from endpoints, network sensors, and user behavior analytics. Security teams should use continuous monitoring to detect anomalies such as unauthorized access, privilege escalation, or unusual traffic flows. Threat detection can be further enhanced through machine learning-based systems that recognize patterns across cloud boundaries, improving detection accuracy while reducing false positives.

Network security strategies must also be adapted to secure multi-cloud and hybrid workloads. Organizations should deploy virtual firewalls, microsegmentation, and software-defined networking (SDN) to enforce granular traffic controls between cloud resources, data centers, and users. Secure connectivity options such as VPNs, direct interconnects, and software-defined WANs (SD-WAN) provide encrypted tunnels for secure communication, while cloud access security brokers (CASBs) offer visibility and control over SaaS application usage. Implementing Zero Trust principles across environments ensures that no user or device is inherently trusted, even when operating within an internal network. Access to resources is granted based on continuous verification of identity, device health, location, and behavior, reducing reliance on traditional network perimeters.

Data protection is another cornerstone of multi-cloud and hybrid security. Data must be encrypted at rest, in transit, and preferably in use, with key management centralized or federated to maintain control across cloud providers. Organizations should implement data classification and labeling to enforce appropriate controls based on sensitivity levels, using data loss prevention (DLP) tools to monitor and block unauthorized sharing or transfers. Secure API gateways and application firewalls should be used to protect public-facing services from injection, denial-of-service, and credential stuffing attacks. Each cloud provider's native security services should be leveraged to their fullest extent, but layered with third-party tools when cross-platform compatibility or deeper analytics are required.

Governance and compliance remain integral to these strategies, especially as regulations such as GDPR, HIPAA, and PCI DSS mandate strict controls over data residency, access auditing, and breach notification. Automated compliance tools should be used to continuously assess configurations, remediate policy violations, and generate audit-ready reports. Policy-as-Code and Infrastructure-as-

Code practices support consistent deployment of secure configurations and simplify compliance tracking. Security teams must work closely with DevOps and cloud architects to embed security into every phase of the deployment lifecycle, using automated testing and validation to enforce security standards without slowing innovation. Multi-cloud and hybrid cloud strategies must be designed for agility, scalability, and resilience, while maintaining uniform security controls that adapt to the diversity and dynamism of modern enterprise environments.

BOOK 4
THREAT DETECTION AND INCIDENT RESPONSE
PROACTIVE DEFENSE STRATEGIES FOR CYBER THREATS

ROB BOTWRIGHT

Chapter 1: Understanding the Threat Landscape

Understanding the threat landscape is fundamental to building an effective cybersecurity strategy, especially as threats continue to evolve in complexity, scope, and scale. In the modern digital environment, threats are no longer confined to isolated malware incidents or opportunistic attacks but have expanded into highly organized, persistent, and targeted campaigns carried out by cybercriminals, nation-state actors, hacktivists, and insiders. The threat landscape includes a wide range of attack vectors, tactics, techniques, and procedures (TTPs) that adversaries use to exploit vulnerabilities, steal data, disrupt operations, or compromise systems for financial, political, or strategic gain. These threats can come from external attackers exploiting software flaws, insiders abusing legitimate access, or third-party vendors introducing risks through insecure integrations and supply chains.

Malware remains one of the most pervasive threats, with variants such as ransomware, spyware, and trojans designed to gain unauthorized access, encrypt files, or exfiltrate data. Ransomware attacks have grown significantly in recent years, shifting from indiscriminate campaigns to highly targeted extortion operations against critical infrastructure, healthcare institutions, and enterprise networks. These attacks often begin with phishing emails, malicious attachments, or the exploitation of unpatched vulnerabilities in exposed systems, and once inside, attackers move laterally, escalate privileges, and deploy encryption across networks while demanding payment for decryption keys. In addition to data encryption, some ransomware operators now exfiltrate data and threaten to publish it unless ransom demands are met, increasing pressure on victims and compounding the damage.

Social engineering is another dominant component of the threat landscape, exploiting human psychology to deceive users into revealing credentials, installing malware, or transferring funds. Phishing remains the most common social engineering technique, often disguised as messages from trusted brands, colleagues, or system notifications. These messages lure recipients into clicking malicious links or entering login details into fraudulent websites. Business email compromise (BEC) attacks are more targeted forms of social engineering where attackers impersonate executives or trusted partners to manipulate employees into executing unauthorized financial transactions or sharing sensitive information. Unlike broad phishing campaigns, BEC attacks rely on research and personalization, making them harder to detect and often more successful.

Advanced persistent threats (APTs) represent some of the most sophisticated dangers in the threat landscape. These long-term, targeted intrusions are typically carried out by well-funded adversaries such as nation-state actors, with objectives ranging from espionage to sabotage. APTs are characterized by their stealth, persistence, and use of custom malware, zero-day vulnerabilities, and multi-stage attack chains. Attackers often establish a foothold through spear-phishing or credential theft, followed by lateral movement, data exfiltration, and ongoing surveillance. The presence of an APT can remain undetected for months or even years, requiring advanced detection tools, threat hunting, and behavioral analytics to uncover.

Insider threats also pose significant risk and are often underestimated. These can be malicious insiders seeking to harm the organization or careless users who unintentionally expose sensitive data through misconfiguration, weak passwords, or poor security hygiene. Insider threats are difficult to detect because the activity often appears legitimate and may involve users with high levels of access. Monitoring user behavior, implementing least privilege access, and maintaining strong audit trails are necessary to mitigate these risks.

The rise of supply chain attacks has further expanded the threat landscape, as attackers target third-party vendors, software dependencies, or update mechanisms to infiltrate otherwise secure organizations. The SolarWinds breach is a high-profile example, where attackers compromised the software build process of a widely used IT management platform, resulting in backdoor access for thousands of organizations. These attacks highlight the importance of securing development pipelines, validating code integrity, and performing thorough risk assessments of partners and vendors.

IoT and cloud environments have also introduced new dimensions to the threat landscape. IoT devices often lack built-in security and are deployed in vast numbers with default credentials or outdated firmware, making them ideal targets for botnets and surveillance. Cloud environments, while scalable and efficient, are susceptible to misconfigurations, exposed APIs, and insecure storage if not properly governed. Understanding the threat landscape requires constant vigilance, threat intelligence integration, and adaptive defenses that evolve with attacker methods, ensuring that organizations remain prepared for both known and emerging risks.

Chapter 2: The Cyber Kill Chain and Attack Lifecycle

The Cyber Kill Chain and the attack lifecycle provide a structured framework for understanding how adversaries plan, execute, and achieve their objectives in a cyberattack, enabling defenders to identify, interrupt, and respond to each stage of an intrusion. Developed by Lockheed Martin, the Cyber Kill Chain outlines seven distinct phases of a typical attack: reconnaissance, weaponization, delivery, exploitation, installation, command and control (C2), and actions on objectives. By dissecting an attack into these phases, organizations gain insights into attacker behavior, improve detection capabilities, and design layered defenses that address each point of the chain. The attack lifecycle, often used interchangeably with the Kill Chain, also emphasizes the iterative and persistent nature of attacks, recognizing that adversaries adapt their methods as they encounter obstacles or detection.

The first phase, reconnaissance, involves the attacker gathering information about the target organization, its systems, personnel, and infrastructure. This step can include scanning for open ports, identifying software versions, and collecting employee details from social media or public records. The attacker's goal is to identify weaknesses that can be exploited in later stages, such as unpatched systems, exposed services, or users who may be vulnerable to phishing. Passive reconnaissance uses publicly available data, while active reconnaissance involves probing the network, which may trigger alerts if proper monitoring is in place.

In the weaponization phase, the attacker creates a malicious payload tailored to the weaknesses identified during reconnaissance. This often includes combining an exploit with a backdoor, trojan, or other malware capable of providing persistent access or stealing data. The payload may be embedded into a document, script, or executable file designed to evade detection by traditional security tools. Weaponization is typically performed in the attacker's environment, allowing them to craft and test the malware before deployment, ensuring a high likelihood of success once delivered.

The delivery phase refers to the method used to transmit the malicious payload to the target. Common delivery vectors include phishing emails, malicious links, drive-by downloads, USB devices, or exploiting exposed services over the internet. Phishing is especially popular due to its low cost and high success rate, often relying on social engineering to trick users into opening attachments or clicking links. Drive-by downloads can occur when a user visits a compromised or malicious website that silently delivers malware without requiring user interaction.

During the exploitation phase, the delivered payload activates by exploiting a vulnerability on the target system. This could involve executing malicious macros in a document, exploiting a browser or plugin vulnerability, or abusing a misconfigured system. Successful exploitation allows the attacker to gain initial access and execute arbitrary code, often escalating privileges to gain deeper access. At this point, if endpoint protection or exploit mitigation tools are not properly configured, the attacker can begin establishing a foothold within the environment.

Installation follows exploitation and involves deploying malware to ensure continued access. This can include keyloggers, rootkits, remote access trojans (RATs), or other tools that provide persistent control over the system. Malware is often installed in a way that avoids detection, such as using fileless techniques or embedding code in legitimate processes. Persistence mechanisms may include registry modifications, scheduled tasks, or manipulation of startup routines, allowing the attacker to maintain access even after reboots or user logouts.

The command and control phase enables the attacker to communicate with the compromised system remotely. C2 servers allow attackers to issue commands, update malware, exfiltrate data, or pivot to other systems within the network. Communication may be encrypted or disguised as legitimate traffic to avoid detection. Some advanced attackers use multiple C2 channels, domain generation algorithms, or peer-to-peer networks to ensure redundancy and resilience against takedown attempts.

In the final phase, actions on objectives, the attacker fulfills their mission, which can vary widely depending on their intent. This may involve stealing intellectual property, harvesting credentials, exfiltrating sensitive data, deploying ransomware, or sabotaging systems. Once the objective is achieved, attackers may maintain persistence for future access or attempt to erase their tracks to avoid detection and forensic analysis. By mapping security incidents to the Kill Chain, defenders can identify which stages were successful, where detection failed, and how to improve controls to disrupt future attacks before they reach critical objectives.

Chapter 3: Indicators of Compromise and Attack

Indicators of Compromise (IOCs) and Indicators of Attack (IOAs) are fundamental components of modern cybersecurity detection and response, helping organizations identify malicious activity within their systems, networks, or cloud environments. IOCs refer to the forensic artifacts that suggest a system has been compromised, including evidence such as file hashes, IP addresses, domain names, URLs, registry changes, malware signatures, and unusual network traffic. These are retrospective in nature, meaning they help analysts confirm that a breach has occurred or is in progress. IOAs, on the other hand, are behavioral signals that focus on the intent and tactics of an attack rather than its digital footprint. IOAs provide a more proactive approach, allowing security teams to detect and disrupt attacks based on patterns of behavior that are characteristic of malicious activity, even if specific IOCs have not yet been observed.

IOCs are commonly used in threat intelligence sharing, allowing organizations and cybersecurity vendors to publish known malicious indicators derived from malware analysis, intrusion investigations, or honeypots. For example, if a malware campaign is discovered using a particular command-and-control domain or dropping a file with a specific hash value, that information can be distributed as an IOC. Security tools such as intrusion detection systems (IDS), firewalls, endpoint detection and response (EDR) platforms, and SIEM systems can then be configured to watch for those indicators across monitored environments. When a match is detected, an alert is generated, prompting an analyst to investigate further. While this method is effective for identifying known threats, it is limited in its ability to detect new or highly customized attacks that do not match existing IOCs.

This limitation is addressed by IOAs, which focus on the underlying tactics, techniques, and procedures (TTPs) that attackers use. Rather than looking for a known file hash or IP address, IOAs identify suspicious sequences of actions such as a legitimate process spawning a command shell, a user account suddenly accessing sensitive resources outside normal business hours, or unusual privilege escalation attempts. These behaviors are analyzed in context, and when patterns emerge that align with known attack methodologies, they raise red flags—even if no specific IOC is present. IOAs enable organizations to detect zero-day threats, living-off-the-land attacks, and fileless malware, which often evade traditional detection methods.

Security platforms that utilize machine learning and behavioral analytics are particularly effective at identifying IOAs. By establishing baselines for normal user and system behavior, they can detect anomalies and chain together related events to create a narrative of an attack in progress. For instance, an IOA-based alert might begin with a user receiving a phishing email, followed by the opening of a malicious attachment, creation of a scheduled task, and connection to an external IP address—all of which might seem benign in isolation but are highly suspicious when observed together. This type of analysis requires the aggregation and correlation of logs and telemetry data from multiple sources, including endpoints, servers, cloud platforms, and identity providers.

The combination of IOCs and IOAs forms a comprehensive detection strategy. IOCs provide concrete, low-level indicators that help confirm incidents and support forensic investigations, while IOAs help detect emerging threats and trigger defensive responses before damage is done. Both types of indicators should be integrated into automated detection tools and continuously updated with current intelligence. Threat feeds from commercial and open-source sources provide IOCs in formats such as STIX, TAXII, or JSON, which can be imported into SIEMs or threat intelligence platforms for enrichment. Meanwhile, IOA-based detections often rely on predefined behavioral rules or machine learning models that evolve as they ingest new data and analyst feedback.

Incident response workflows rely on both IOCs and IOAs for prioritizing alerts, scoping the impact of attacks, and initiating remediation. IOCs help trace the spread of malware or identify exfiltration points, while IOAs indicate attacker intent and help security teams understand how far the adversary has progressed along the kill chain. Maintaining up-to-date threat intelligence, tuning detection rules, and analyzing historical data for both indicators strengthens an organization's ability to prevent, detect, and respond to a constantly evolving threat landscape.

Chapter 4: Building an Effective Detection Strategy

Building an effective detection strategy requires a deep understanding of the threat landscape, the organization's unique risk profile, and the tools and techniques available to detect malicious activity across infrastructure, applications, endpoints, users, and data. Detection is not just about finding known threats but also identifying anomalies, suspicious behavior, and previously unseen attack techniques that may indicate compromise. A comprehensive strategy begins with establishing visibility across all relevant environments, including on-premises systems, cloud platforms, remote endpoints, SaaS applications, and third-party integrations. Without consistent and reliable visibility, detection efforts are limited in scope and prone to gaps that attackers can exploit.

Central to any detection strategy is the ability to collect and analyze data from a wide variety of sources. This includes endpoint telemetry, network traffic, application logs, authentication events, cloud service activity, and system changes. A Security Information and Event Management (SIEM) system serves as the backbone of this effort, aggregating and correlating logs in real time, applying rules to identify indicators of compromise or attack, and generating alerts for further investigation. The quality and completeness of the data ingested into the SIEM directly affect the effectiveness of detection. To ensure data fidelity, organizations must standardize log formats, normalize fields, and apply timestamps and source identifiers consistently across environments.

Detection rules and use cases must be aligned with the organization's threat model, which includes the most likely attack vectors, adversary tactics, and potential impact of an incident. For example, organizations in the financial sector may prioritize detection of credential theft, fraudulent transactions, and insider threats, while healthcare organizations may focus on unauthorized access to patient data and ransomware activity. The MITRE ATT&CK framework is an invaluable tool for mapping known adversary techniques to detection logic. By aligning detections with specific ATT&CK techniques, security teams can identify coverage gaps, measure maturity, and ensure their controls are relevant to real-world threats.

Behavior-based detection is a key component of a modern detection strategy. While signature-based approaches are useful for identifying known malware or threat indicators, they are ineffective against zero-day attacks, fileless malware, or sophisticated adversaries using legitimate tools for malicious purposes. Behavioral analytics leverages baselines of normal activity to detect deviations, such as unusual login patterns, abnormal data transfers, or atypical command execution. This requires the integration of machine learning or statistical models into detection platforms, enabling dynamic evaluation of user and system behavior over time. Threats that blend into the environment, such as living-off-the-land attacks, can be identified through subtle patterns that traditional detection methods may overlook.

To reduce alert fatigue and improve response efficiency, detection strategies must include prioritization, tuning, and contextual enrichment. Not all alerts carry the same risk, and raw alerts without context can overwhelm security analysts. Integrating threat intelligence into the detection pipeline enhances the fidelity of alerts by adding context about known malicious actors, IP addresses, domains, and malware signatures. Threat intelligence feeds should be both external—sourced from trusted vendors and open communities—and internal, generated from previous incidents and ongoing investigations. Alerts should be scored based on severity, potential impact, and the confidence level of the detection logic, enabling security teams to focus on the most pressing issues.

Automation also plays a critical role in an effective detection strategy. Security Orchestration, Automation, and Response (SOAR) tools allow for automated triage, investigation, and even containment actions when certain conditions are met. For instance, an alert indicating a known malicious file hash on an endpoint could automatically trigger isolation of the device, blocking of the associated domain, and ticket creation for analyst review. These workflows reduce response times, free up analyst resources, and ensure consistent handling of recurring incidents. Continuous feedback loops, where analysts review detections and adjust rules or models based on their findings, help improve accuracy and reduce false positives over time.

A mature detection strategy also requires regular testing and validation. This includes red teaming, purple teaming, and adversary emulation exercises to determine whether detection logic works as intended against realistic attack scenarios. Using tools like MITRE's CALDERA or Atomic Red Team, security teams can simulate various attack techniques and measure how effectively their systems detect them. Metrics such as detection coverage, mean time to detect (MTTD), and false positive rates help guide improvements and demonstrate the effectiveness of the detection program to stakeholders.

Chapter 5: Leveraging SIEM and SOAR Platforms

Leveraging SIEM and SOAR platforms is a critical component of modern cybersecurity operations, allowing organizations to enhance visibility, accelerate incident response, and manage the increasing volume and complexity of security events across hybrid and multi-cloud environments. Security Information and Event Management (SIEM) systems serve as centralized hubs for collecting, aggregating, and analyzing log data from a wide range of sources including endpoints, servers, firewalls, intrusion detection systems, cloud services, identity providers, and applications. This log data is normalized, correlated, and evaluated against detection rules to identify patterns that may indicate security incidents such as unauthorized access, malware infections, privilege escalation, or data exfiltration. SIEM platforms enable security analysts to visualize activity across the environment, investigate alerts, generate reports, and maintain audit trails for compliance.

The effectiveness of a SIEM platform depends on its ability to ingest high-quality data from relevant sources, normalize it into a usable format, and apply correlation logic that connects related events across different systems. For example, a successful login from an unusual location followed by file access and privilege escalation on a domain controller may not trigger individual alarms, but when these events are linked by a SIEM, they reveal a potential attack in progress. Rule-based detection engines within SIEMs allow organizations to define specific use cases aligned with their threat models, while threat intelligence integrations enrich log data with known indicators of compromise such as malicious IP addresses, file hashes, or domains. This contextual information increases the accuracy and severity of alerts, helping analysts prioritize their investigations.

As organizations face growing alert volumes and limited security resources, the need for automation and orchestration becomes clear. This is where Security Orchestration, Automation, and Response (SOAR) platforms come into play. SOAR platforms integrate with SIEMs and other security tools to automate repetitive tasks, streamline workflows, and enable consistent, documented incident response processes. When an alert is generated by the SIEM, the SOAR platform can initiate a predefined playbook that executes actions such as gathering additional context, querying threat intelligence sources, isolating affected endpoints, blocking IP addresses at the firewall, or opening tickets in an IT service management system. These automated responses reduce the time it takes to contain threats and allow analysts to focus on more complex tasks that require human judgment.

Playbooks within SOAR platforms are customizable and can be adapted to specific threat scenarios, compliance requirements, or organizational policies. For example, a phishing email detection playbook might extract indicators from the message, scan internal mailboxes for similar emails, disable compromised user accounts, and notify affected employees—all without manual intervention. Playbooks can also include conditional logic to branch into different actions based on the severity of the alert or the presence of specific attributes. By automating triage and remediation steps, SOAR platforms help reduce mean time to detect (MTTD) and mean time to respond (MTTR), which are key performance indicators for security operations centers.

The combination of SIEM and SOAR provides a powerful foundation for threat detection and response. SIEM acts as the brain that analyzes and correlates data, while SOAR acts as the muscle that carries out the response. Together, they enable a proactive security posture where threats are identified, verified, and addressed in near real-time.

Continuous tuning of detection rules in the SIEM and regular updates to SOAR playbooks ensure that both platforms remain aligned with evolving threats and business needs. Integration between SIEM and SOAR with other tools such as endpoint detection and response (EDR), cloud security platforms, and vulnerability scanners further enhances the capability to detect, assess, and neutralize threats across the entire technology stack.

Metrics and dashboards from SIEM and SOAR platforms also provide valuable insights for reporting and improvement. Security leaders can use these metrics to understand trends, demonstrate compliance, identify bottlenecks, and justify investments. By operationalizing detection and response through SIEM and SOAR, organizations can scale their security operations, improve efficiency, and build resilience against the growing sophistication of cyber threats.

Chapter 6: Real-Time Monitoring and Alert Tuning

Real-time monitoring and alert tuning are essential practices in any modern cybersecurity operations strategy, providing the necessary visibility and control to detect and respond to threats as they unfold across an organization's digital environment. As networks expand across cloud platforms, remote endpoints, data centers, and SaaS applications, security teams must be able to continuously monitor logs, events, and telemetry in real time to identify indicators of compromise, policy violations, or unusual activity that may suggest malicious intent. Real-time monitoring enables security operations centers (SOCs) to identify threats in their early stages, often before damage is done, but to be truly effective, this monitoring must be paired with carefully tuned alerts that balance sensitivity with accuracy to avoid alert fatigue and ensure actionable insights.

Monitoring begins with comprehensive data collection from across the entire technology stack, including endpoints, network devices, cloud infrastructure, identity providers, authentication systems, application logs, and third-party integrations. The volume of data generated is massive, and to manage it effectively, organizations rely on Security Information and Event Management (SIEM) platforms that ingest, normalize, correlate, and analyze this information. These platforms enable real-time detection by applying rules and analytics to streaming data, flagging events that match known attack patterns or deviate from established baselines of normal activity. However, not all events are threats, and without tuning, the SIEM may produce thousands of alerts, many of which are false positives or of low relevance, overwhelming analysts and increasing the risk that genuine threats go unnoticed.

Alert tuning is the process of refining detection rules, thresholds, and filters so that alerts are meaningful, prioritized, and relevant to the organization's risk profile. This involves analyzing the results of existing alerts, identifying noise patterns, adjusting sensitivity levels, and applying contextual filters such as asset criticality, user behavior baselines, or time-of-day logic. For example, a brute-force login alert might be valid when targeting an administrator account during off-hours, but irrelevant if triggered by a misconfigured script during routine maintenance. Tuning this rule to exclude known safe conditions reduces noise while maintaining security. Threat intelligence feeds can be integrated to enrich alerts with data about known malicious indicators, helping analysts distinguish between benign anomalies and active threats.

Risk-based alerting is a key outcome of effective tuning, allowing alerts to be scored and prioritized based on the value of the asset, the likelihood of compromise, and the potential impact. A single failed login attempt may not warrant action, but when combined with other behaviors such as a rare geolocation, new device fingerprint, or lateral movement, the system can raise the alert priority. This contextual awareness helps security teams focus their efforts on the most critical threats rather than being distracted by low-priority events. Machine learning and behavioral analytics further enhance this process by dynamically adjusting thresholds and identifying evolving patterns of suspicious activity without relying solely on static rules.

Continuous improvement is essential in real-time monitoring and alert tuning. As new threats emerge and environments evolve, detection rules must be reviewed and updated regularly to remain effective. Feedback loops from incident response teams are valuable for identifying gaps in detection, fine-tuning rule parameters, and improving false positive rates. In some cases, creating custom detection rules tailored to the organization's infrastructure, business operations, or known threat scenarios can improve precision far more than relying on generic vendor-provided content. Regular tuning sessions, supported by metrics such as alert volume, true positive rate, mean time to detect, and analyst workload, help optimize the signal-to-noise ratio and ensure the monitoring system remains efficient and focused.

Collaboration between detection engineers, SOC analysts, and incident responders is also crucial in refining alerts and response workflows. Analysts can provide real-world insights into which alerts are most useful, while detection engineers adjust rules based on operational impact. This teamwork creates a more agile detection environment where rule changes are responsive to actual threats and evolving tactics. Automation can assist by tagging alerts, initiating enrichment queries, or routing events based on severity, helping streamline triage and reduce manual effort. Real-time monitoring paired with well-tuned alerts gives organizations the ability to stay ahead of threats, respond decisively, and maintain control over complex, fast-moving digital environments.

Chapter 7: Incident Response Planning and Playbooks

Incident response planning and playbooks are foundational elements of a mature cybersecurity program, enabling organizations to prepare for, manage, and recover from security incidents with speed, consistency, and efficiency. In today's rapidly evolving threat landscape, where organizations face a broad spectrum of cyberattacks ranging from ransomware and phishing to data breaches and insider threats, having a well-defined and tested incident response plan is essential to minimize business disruption, contain damage, and ensure compliance with legal and regulatory requirements. An incident response plan provides the overarching strategy and structure for how an organization responds to cybersecurity events, while playbooks translate that strategy into detailed, step-by-step procedures for specific types of incidents.

A comprehensive incident response plan begins with the identification of key stakeholders and the establishment of roles and responsibilities. This includes not only technical responders such as SOC analysts and IT administrators but also legal counsel, communications teams, compliance officers, and executive leadership. Clear escalation paths must be defined so that incidents are communicated to the appropriate levels of the organization based on severity, impact, and business risk. The plan should specify how incidents are classified—such as low, medium, or high priority—based on criteria such as data sensitivity, system criticality, scope of compromise, or potential regulatory exposure. These classifications guide decision-making throughout the response process and determine the urgency of containment and remediation efforts.

Preparation also includes ensuring that communication channels are secure and accessible during an incident, especially if systems are compromised. Out-of-band communication methods, such as encrypted messaging platforms or offline contact lists, should be in place to coordinate response efforts safely. Contact information for external partners, such as managed security service providers, incident response consultants, law enforcement, and regulatory bodies, should be documented and readily available. Regular training, tabletop exercises, and red team simulations help teams practice their roles and refine procedures, increasing readiness and reducing the chance of error during real-world incidents.

Incident response playbooks are detailed guides that define the specific actions to take when a particular type of threat is detected. Each playbook outlines the tools, techniques, and procedures (TTPs) required for detection, triage, containment, eradication, recovery, and post-incident analysis. For example, a phishing email playbook might include steps for identifying malicious emails in user inboxes, isolating affected endpoints, resetting compromised credentials, and analyzing email headers and attachments for IOCs. A ransomware playbook would involve steps for shutting down infected systems, blocking network access to command and control servers, restoring data from backups, and notifying affected stakeholders. Playbooks help standardize responses, reduce decision-making under pressure, and ensure that critical steps are not overlooked.

Playbooks also integrate with security tools such as SIEMs, SOAR platforms, and EDR solutions to automate portions of the response workflow. When a phishing email is detected by the SIEM, for instance, a SOAR platform can trigger a playbook that extracts indicators from the email, searches for similar messages, quarantines affected mailboxes, and alerts the security team. Automation increases speed and consistency while reducing the manual workload for analysts, but human oversight remains essential for complex or ambiguous situations. Playbooks should include branching logic to account for different scenarios, such as whether the compromise is confirmed, whether data was exfiltrated, or whether legal notification thresholds have been reached.

Post-incident analysis is a critical component of every playbook, ensuring that lessons learned are documented and applied to improve future responses. This includes root cause analysis, timeline reconstruction, assessment of detection and response effectiveness, and identification of areas for improvement in tooling, processes, or communication. Findings should be shared with relevant stakeholders, and updates to playbooks or the broader incident response plan should be made promptly. By continuously refining incident response planning and playbooks based on real-world experience, threat intelligence, and changing infrastructure, organizations can maintain a high level of preparedness and resilience against cyber threats.

Chapter 8: Containment, Eradication, and Recovery

Containment, eradication, and recovery are critical phases within the incident response lifecycle, forming the structured process that organizations follow after identifying a security incident in order to limit its spread, eliminate the root cause, and restore systems to normal operations. These steps are essential for minimizing business disruption, protecting sensitive data, and preventing attackers from regaining access or causing further harm. Once an incident is confirmed during the detection and analysis phase, the next priority becomes containment, which involves taking swift action to isolate the threat and stop it from moving laterally across systems, accessing additional data, or impacting more users or services. Containment strategies vary depending on the scope and severity of the incident, but they often include network segmentation, blocking malicious IP addresses or domains, isolating affected endpoints, disabling compromised accounts, and applying firewall rules to prevent outbound communication with known command and control servers.

Containment can be short-term or long-term, with short-term measures designed to immediately halt the spread of the threat and long-term measures focused on maintaining business continuity while preparing for eradication. For example, in the case of a ransomware outbreak, short-term containment may involve disconnecting infected machines from the network, while long-term containment could include implementing stricter access controls, restricting administrative privileges, or redirecting user traffic through secured gateways to prevent re-infection. During this phase, it is essential to collect forensic evidence such as memory dumps, network logs, and file system snapshots before making changes to the affected systems, as this data will support the investigation and may be needed for regulatory reporting or legal action.

Once the threat has been contained and its behavior understood, the eradication phase focuses on identifying and removing all malicious artifacts, such as malware, scripts, backdoors, unauthorized accounts, and registry changes that the attacker may have left behind. This process often includes scanning systems with antivirus and endpoint detection and response (EDR) tools, performing manual analysis to detect hidden persistence mechanisms, and validating the integrity of system files and configurations. If the attack involved exploitation of a software vulnerability, patching the affected systems or disabling the vulnerable service is a critical step in eradication. In some cases, reimaging infected machines or rebuilding compromised servers from known-good backups is the most effective way to ensure complete removal of the threat.

Throughout the eradication phase, teams must coordinate with system owners and affected departments to minimize operational impact and verify that all affected components have been identified and addressed. Communication is essential, both within the incident response team and with external stakeholders, to maintain situational awareness and ensure a smooth transition into the recovery phase. Once eradication is complete and systems are deemed clean, the recovery phase begins, focusing on restoring business operations and returning systems to a fully functional and secure state. Recovery involves restoring data from clean backups, re-enabling services, validating system functionality, and monitoring systems closely for signs of lingering threats or reinfection.

Recovery plans must also include steps to reinforce system security, such as applying hardened configurations, updating passwords, reissuing authentication tokens, and implementing additional monitoring controls. In cloud and hybrid environments, recovery may include redeploying infrastructure as code from secure templates and validating the security posture of cloud workloads. During recovery, user access may be gradually restored based on risk level and business priority, with high-value assets and critical services prioritized for restoration. Continuous monitoring should remain active throughout this period to detect any anomalies or indicators that the attacker may still have access or that the original infection vector has not been fully mitigated.

In parallel with technical recovery, organizations must manage reputational risk, legal obligations, and compliance requirements by documenting actions taken, notifying regulators if necessary, and communicating transparently with customers, partners, or the public. A well-documented post-incident review process ensures that all findings are captured, root causes identified, and lessons learned incorporated into future incident response plans, detection rules, and security controls. This process helps strengthen the organization's security posture and ensures that containment, eradication, and recovery efforts are continuously refined to address new threats, infrastructure changes, and evolving business needs.

Chapter 9: Post-Incident Analysis and Threat Hunting

Post-incident analysis and threat hunting are vital components of a proactive cybersecurity program, providing organizations with the means to understand the root causes of security incidents, improve defenses, and uncover hidden threats that may not have triggered traditional detection mechanisms. After an incident has been contained, eradicated, and recovery is complete, post-incident analysis begins by reconstructing the timeline of events to determine how the attack was executed, which systems were affected, and what vulnerabilities or misconfigurations were exploited. This process includes gathering and correlating logs from endpoints, servers, network devices, cloud platforms, and authentication systems to piece together the attacker's movements, from initial access through lateral movement, privilege escalation, data exfiltration, or persistence mechanisms. Analysts examine how detection and response processes performed, assess whether alerts were generated in time, and evaluate whether any opportunities for earlier detection were missed.

Root cause analysis is a central objective of post-incident activities, as identifying the origin of an attack helps prevent recurrence and reveals weaknesses in controls, procedures, or technology. For example, if an incident originated from a phishing email, analysts may review the email gateway rules, user training effectiveness, and endpoint behavior following the malicious link. If attackers exploited an unpatched vulnerability, the investigation may focus on patch management practices, asset inventory completeness, and vulnerability scanning frequency. Detailed documentation of findings is critical, including the timeline of attacker activity, the attack vector, affected systems, data at risk, containment steps taken, and recommendations for improvement. These reports not only support internal learning but may also be required for regulatory reporting, insurance claims, or legal investigations.

Lessons learned meetings should involve not only security teams but also IT, legal, compliance, communications, and executive leadership to ensure that insights are shared across the organization. These sessions help validate whether the incident response plan and playbooks were followed correctly, highlight gaps in coordination, and identify areas where additional training or tooling may be needed. The outcome of post-incident analysis should drive actionable changes, such as updating detection rules, refining playbooks, improving logging coverage, enhancing alert tuning, or implementing additional security controls. These improvements feed back into the incident response lifecycle and strengthen the organization's resilience against future threats. Threat hunting complements post-incident analysis by taking a proactive approach to finding adversaries or malicious activity that has not yet been detected. While post-incident analysis focuses on known events, threat hunting assumes that attackers may already be inside the environment and that existing security controls may have failed to detect them. Threat hunters use hypotheses based on threat intelligence, attacker behavior, or observed anomalies to guide their searches across logs, endpoint telemetry, and network traffic. They look for signs of lateral movement, command and control activity, unusual file or process behavior, suspicious authentication patterns, and other subtle indicators that traditional detection systems might overlook.

Effective threat hunting relies on a combination of skilled analysts, rich telemetry, and flexible tools for querying and analysis. Platforms such as SIEMs, EDRs, and security analytics solutions provide the necessary visibility, while frameworks like MITRE

ATT&CK help guide hunts by mapping tactics and techniques to specific data sources. Threat hunting efforts can be reactive, triggered by alerts or incidents, or proactive, scheduled as part of continuous security operations. Each hunt should be documented and reviewed to capture findings, update detection rules, and refine hypotheses based on what was discovered or ruled out. Successful threat hunting can uncover dormant threats, misconfigured systems, or indicators of compromise that were previously unknown. It also helps validate the effectiveness of current detection capabilities and often leads to the development of new detection logic that can be automated going forward. Threat hunting teams may also conduct purple teaming exercises with red team members to simulate attacker behavior and test the organization's ability to detect it. These exercises reveal how well visibility, detection, and response mechanisms work in practice and highlight areas that require investment or improvement. By combining deep forensic analysis after incidents with continuous, intelligence-driven threat hunting, organizations gain a more complete and proactive understanding of their threat environment and are better equipped to defend against both current and emerging attacks.

Chapter 10: Building a Culture of Continuous Readines

Building a culture of continuous readiness in cybersecurity requires an organization-wide mindset that treats security not as a one-time initiative or a reactionary measure, but as an ongoing, integral part of every process, decision, and digital interaction. In an era where threats evolve rapidly and attackers exploit both technical vulnerabilities and human behavior, a static or compliance-only approach to security is insufficient. Continuous readiness means that every individual, from executive leadership to entry-level employees, understands their role in protecting information systems and is equipped with the tools, knowledge, and awareness to act effectively. This culture starts with strong leadership support, where security is positioned not as a barrier to innovation but as a foundational enabler of trust, resilience, and long-term business continuity.

Executive buy-in is essential for embedding security into strategic objectives and allocating the necessary resources for ongoing readiness. Leadership must actively promote security values, support risk-based decision-making, and prioritize long-term investments in tools, training, and personnel that support proactive defense. Security leaders should be present in boardroom discussions, helping stakeholders understand the business impact of cyber risk and the value of a mature security posture. With leadership aligned, the next step is to embed security into every phase of the organizational lifecycle, including product development, procurement, HR policies, third-party risk management, and customer engagement.

A culture of continuous readiness thrives on collaboration between departments. Security cannot operate in isolation or be perceived as solely the responsibility of the IT or cybersecurity team. Cross-functional collaboration ensures that developers adopt secure coding practices, network engineers design resilient infrastructure, HR enforces secure onboarding and offboarding procedures, and finance monitors for fraudulent transactions. Security champions can be appointed within each department to act as liaisons who promote best practices, identify risks unique to their area, and provide feedback to the central security team. This decentralized approach increases visibility, distributes responsibility, and helps scale readiness across diverse business functions.

Ongoing education and awareness are core pillars of continuous readiness. Employees must receive regular training on security fundamentals such as phishing awareness, password hygiene, data classification, and incident reporting. These programs should evolve with the threat landscape and use engaging formats such as simulations, gamification, and interactive workshops to reinforce learning. Security awareness should not be limited to annual compliance checklists but delivered as an ongoing conversation that keeps cybersecurity top of mind. This includes internal newsletters, threat briefings, tabletop exercises, and instant feedback when employees encounter suspicious activity. Empowering staff to recognize and report threats makes them active participants in the defense of the organization.

Operationally, continuous readiness requires robust processes for detection, response, and recovery. Threats must be continuously monitored through SIEM, EDR, and other analytics tools, with alerts tuned for relevance and playbooks maintained for rapid response. Incident response drills should be conducted regularly to ensure that teams can execute under pressure and adapt plans based on lessons learned. Vulnerability management must be continuous, with automated scanning, patch deployment, and prioritization based on business impact. Change management processes should include security assessments as standard checkpoints to identify risks before they are introduced into production environments.

Metrics and measurement are also necessary for sustaining readiness. Organizations must track key performance indicators such as mean time to detect, mean time to respond, false positive rates, patch latency, and user engagement with training. These metrics help security leaders identify areas of improvement, justify investments, and demonstrate progress over time. Metrics should be transparent and shared with stakeholders to reinforce accountability and foster a data-driven approach to decision-making. Continuous readiness also involves staying aligned with external developments, including emerging threats, regulatory changes, new technologies, and shifts in the business landscape.

Adopting a mindset of continuous readiness means accepting that security is never fully complete but must evolve as the organization grows, as threats change, and as technology advances. This mindset encourages agility, resilience, and a proactive posture where every individual and process contributes to a security-conscious culture. From executives approving budgets for advanced detection tools to end users reporting phishing attempts, every action reinforces the collective readiness of the organization to defend against and recover from modern cyber threats.

Conclusion

As the digital landscape continues to evolve at unprecedented speed, organizations must reimagine security as a continuous, adaptive function—deeply embedded into every layer of their cloud and network ecosystems. Throughout this series, *Cloud Defense: Advanced Endpoint Protection and Secure Network Strategies*, we have explored the foundational principles, practical tools, and forward-looking strategies required to protect today's dynamic environments from increasingly sophisticated cyber threats.

In **Book 1**, we laid the groundwork by establishing secure network architecture principles that emphasize resilience, segmentation, identity-aware access, and cloud-native design. These foundational elements are not just technical implementations but strategic decisions that influence how risk is managed across infrastructure at scale.

Book 2 shifted the focus to the endpoints—the critical edge where users interact with systems and where attackers often strike first. By mastering endpoint protection, organizations can transform vulnerable devices into hardened assets, capable of withstanding modern threats through layered defense, intelligent detection, and user awareness.

In **Book 3**, we turned our attention to defending the cloud perimeter, recognizing that in a world of remote access, SaaS platforms, and API-driven services, the perimeter is no longer a fixed boundary but a flexible, identity-based control surface. Best practices for securing cloud-native infrastructure, enforcing zero trust principles, and managing multi-cloud visibility are now essential components of any mature security strategy.

Book 4 brought the series full circle by focusing on real-time threat detection, incident response, and recovery. In today's climate, it is not a question of if an incident will occur, but when—and how well prepared the organization is to detect, contain, and respond. Proactive defense strategies, supported by intelligent tooling, automation, and a culture of continuous readiness, are the key to maintaining operational integrity and minimizing impact.

Security is no longer a static checklist—it is a living, evolving discipline. It requires a commitment to visibility, adaptability, and collaboration across teams, technologies, and processes. As threat actors continue to advance in sophistication, so too must our defenses evolve in complexity, agility, and depth. The practices and strategies outlined in this series provide a blueprint not only for securing today's environments but for building the resilience needed to face tomorrow's challenges. Defending the cloud requires more than tools—it demands strategy, discipline, and an organizational culture that treats security as a shared responsibility. With these insights, the journey toward secure, agile, and resilient infrastructure continues—not as a final destination, but as a commitment to excellence in every layer of defense.

www.ingramcontent.com/pod-product-compliance
Lightning Source LLC
Chambersburg PA
CBHW071244050326
40690CB00011B/2263